AN INTRODUCTION TO

BUDDHIST ESOTERISM

AN INTRODUCTION TO
BUDDHIST ESOTERISM

BY

BENOYTOSH BHATTACHARYYA

GYAN

Published by

GYAN

Gyan Publishing House
5, Ansari Road
Daryaganj, New Delhi-110002
Phone: 011-47034999, 9811692060
E-mail: books@gyanbooks.com

Distribution Network
gyanbooks.com
India, USA, Canada, UK, Australia

ISBN: 978-93-6280-374-0 (PB)
First Published, 1932

2nd Impression 2024

Printed at: Gyan Press, Delhi.

AN INTRODUCTION TO BUDDHIST ESOTERISM
Author: BENOYTOSH BHATTACHARYYA

AN INTRODUCTION TO BUDDHIST ESOTERISM

PLATE I

KHASARPAṆA LOKEŚVARA

AN INTRODUCTION TO
BUDDHIST ESOTERISM

By

BENOYTOSH BHATTACHARYYA

M.A., Ph.D., *Rājaratna*, *Tattvavācaspati*

Ex-Director, Oriental Institute, Baroda

TO THE SACRED MEMORY
OF MY FATHER

न जायते म्रियते वा कदाचित्
नायं भूत्वा भविता वा न भूयः ।
अजो नित्यः शाश्वतोऽयं पुराणो
न हन्यते हन्यमाने शरीरे ॥

PREFACE

IF at any time in the history of India the mind of the nation as a whole has been diseased, it was in the Tāntric age, or the period immediately preceding the Muhammadan conquest of India. The story related in the pages of the numerous Tāntric works is supposed to be so repugnant that, excepting a few, all respectable scholars have condemned them wholesale and left the field of Tantras severely alone. But in spite of what the great historians of Sanskrit literature have said against Tāntrism and the Tāntric literature, no one should forget that the Hindu population of India as a whole is even today in the grip of this very Tantra in its daily life, customs and usages, and is suffering from the same disease which originated 1,300 years ago and consumed its vitality slowly but surely during these long centuries. Someone should therefore take up the study comprising the diagnosis, ætiology, pathology and prognosis of the disease, so that more capable men may take up its treatment and eradication in the future. The present work represents the first instalment of a series of investigations into this fascinating branch of study, and an attempt to place before scholars a dispassionate account of the Tantras in general, and Buddhist Tantras in particular.[1]

Acknowledgments are here made of the splendid help rendered by Dr. Helen M. Johnson, of Osceola, U.S.A., in revising the manuscript very carefully and conscientiously, and for generously offering valuable advice. Indeed, I feel very deeply indebted to her for all the sympathy and encouragement she freely bestowed on me during her stay in India.

[1] Numerous articles on this subject have been contributed by me to Journals of learned societies and other publications, and many of these are here incorporated for a connected account.

I had a great desire to dedicate this book to my father, the late Mahamahopadhyaya Haraprasād Śāstrī, but as he left us all to mourn his loss during the time this book was passing through the press, I can only inscribe this volume to his sacred memory.

Baroda
March 18, 1931

B. BHATTACHARYYA

CONTENTS

ILLUSTRATIONS

CHAPTER I

INTRODUCTORY

TĀNTRISM originated from primitive magic. The primitive people of India, like all other primitive and nomadic races throughout the world, must have had the primitive magical practices prevalent among them. They had many natural and unnatural enemies to overcome and many unforeseen difficulties to tide over, especially because they had to live like wild animals, in jungles and forests. They could overcome only a small fraction of their distress by using their physical force and their primitive intelligence; but the rest they were powerless to overcome, and these inspired them with superstitious awe and fear. In the physical sphere they were greatly afraid of wild animals, snakes, calamities of nature, diseases, and so forth, which it was not in their power to overcome at all. The common people, afflicted by these dangers, flocked around their sorcerer, who had gifts superior to the ordinary folk. But the sorcerer also being an ordinary mortal was not found always equal to the occasion; and thus the primitive people were inspired with greater awe and fear. In the intellectual sphere, on the other hand, fear of death and of spirits and ghosts exercised the minds of the primitive people to a far greater extent than at present.

It is in this fear that magic, mysticism, sorcery and necromancy had their origin. As the primitive people began to be more and more civilized, they wanted to do something to allay this superstitious fear; and in their attempt to do this they laid the foundation of magic, which in its turn gave rise to the more advanced sciences. To protect themselves from wild animals they had recourse to amulets and charms; against snakes and snake-bites the sorcerers gave them charms and herbs; against diseases they discovered the various crude drugs from plants, leaves and minerals. It was in this way that the primitive people attempted to protect themselves against their natural and supernatural enemies.

When the primitive inhabitants of India were developing a sort of magical system, with a large number of magical practices, they came in contact with the Aryans, who came from the west in large numbers in several waves of migrations. They had natural advantages over the primitive inhabitants of India, because they were strong and intelligent and because they carried with them a sort of civilization. It is difficult at this stage to determine exactly the nature of their civilization; but from the references in their literature, which later on came to be regarded as the four Vedas, it can be seen that they led a sort of nomadic life, moving about from place to place like the herds of animals. As has been said already, there were several waves of migrations, and the Aryan people involved in each migration penetrated further and further towards the east, conquering the primitive inhabitants and reducing them to the position of serfs. They settled in the most convenient places, where there was enough of water and food available, lived like lords by exploiting the labours of the primitive people, and set up independent governments run mostly on republican lines. One such migration settled in the Doab, between the Ganges and the Jumna, and developed a sort of social hierarchy and divided itself into four castes, Brāhmaṇas, Kṣattriyas, Vaiśyas and Śūdras. In striking a line of demarcation amongst the four castes the principle followed was that of the division of labour. Those who had an intellectual bent of mind were regarded as Brāhmaṇas; those who were strong, heroic and of a fighting nature were called Kṣattriyas; those who betook themselves to agriculture and commerce were called Vaiśyas; and the primitive people, who were content to serve these three higher castes ungrudgingly and who followed the rules and regulations laid down by the new society, were called Śūdras. In the course of time, when this experiment of caste system[1] was well established, it was no longer considered as an experiment, but taken as a settled fact. The Aryans of previous and later migrations were called Vrātyas. These Vrātyas were so called because they moved about in hordes, or *vrātyās*, in a primitive fashion; and resembled more or less the other nomadic tribes. The orthodox Aryans, who built up for the first time a grand structure of social hierarchy, were nevertheless conscious that the Vrātyas were their brethren, and they felt a necessity for incorporating them into their own fold.[2] In order to accomplish their object, they convened large congregations of people and performed certain sacrifices, called the Vrātyastomas, in which large numbers of Vrātyas were taken into the orthodox fold on the simple condition that they should relinquish their nomadic habits and dress and take to a settled form of existence. The Aryan settlers of India came with a large number of preconceived notions, dogmas, various philosophical speculations, and magical practices in the form of sacrifices; and, because of these, they were able to exercise a tremendous influence on the primitive inhabitants of the place.

The primitive inhabitants, who were called Dasyus by the Aryans, and sometimes Śūdras, also did not fail to exercise a considerable influence over their white superiors. It is in this way that one reacted on the other, and both were benefited to a certain extent and demoralized also to a certain extent, in

[1] Caste appears to be a purely Indian product. Had it been of still earlier origin we should have expected some sort of caste system amongst the Iranian people.

[2] For this Vrātya theory and the significance of the Vrātyastoma I am much indebted to Mm. Haraprasād Śāstrī, with whom I have had several discussions. The most illuminating paper on this subject has been published by the same author in the *Proceedings of the Asiatic Society of Bengal*, N.S. Vol. XVII, 1921, p. 1 A.

accordance with the intensity of their respective influences. The Aryans came with their Vedic chants and sacrifices, and the primitive people taught them how to live in a strange country and how to protect themselves against the difficulties peculiar to the place itself.

The Aryans brought with them, as is well-known to all, a super-sacrificial system. They were accustomed to perform some sort of sacrifice before commencing any important action. The sacrifices were performed both for physical and spiritual gains. They were of various kinds: some lasted for a few hours and some were carried on for a number of years; some required a few priests only and some required a huge number of them. There were elaborate rules and regulations for the performance of these sacrifices, and it was stipulated that if the sacrifices could be performed in strict accordance with the rules and regulations, their results were most surely obtained. But, as a matter of fact, the rules for the performance of such sacrifices were so elaborate and so minute—the very method of the pronunciation of the letters of the Vedic mantras was so intricate, and had such minute differences—that it was almost humanly impossible either to perform the sacrifices correctly or to pronounce the letters of the mantras accurately. Modern investigators of ancient history designate the sacrifices as instances of a purely primitive form of magic[1] designed in order that those who performed the sacrifices should gain an importance over the other members of the community in the same way as the sorcerers commanded an uncanny influence over the aboriginals. The result was inevitable. The priests, who busied themselves with the sacrifices with ceaseless regularity, were looked upon as the most intelligent people

[1] Dr. Das Gupta thinks otherwise; he considers these as a repository of cosmic secrets and cosmic forces. It is, however, absurd to think that primitive people could realize and discover such secrets and forces when in a practically aboriginal state. See S. N. Das Gupta, *Hindu Mysticism*, pp. 9–10.

amongst the Aryans, and they formed a class amongst themselves as Brāhmaṇas, who exerted a tremendous influence over the Hindu community in those olden days and who continue to exert the same kind of influence even at the present moment.

We cannot call the performance of these sacrifices anything like science, as results to be obtained therefrom were either not obtained at all or were obtained by mere accident. Nor was this religion, because the sacrifices were a sort of revolt against nature. When, in the ordinary course of events, for instance, a king had no child even after many years, he directly engaged a large number of priests, well-known for their abilities, and on payment of fees requested them to hold the Putreṣṭi sacrifice. Here the sacrificers were required to change the natural course of events, which was ordained by God, who is the very essence of all religions. When a man, for instance, engages priests and requests them to perform a sacrifice so that he may proceed to heaven on his demise, the process cannot but be designated as a sort of sacrificial mysticism; because it is not within human power to ascertain whether the given cause gives rise to the expected result or not. The Aryans, before forming themselves into a well-organized caste system, brought with them certain chants and songs, mainly addressed to the elements of nature or the supposed presiding deities of the different natural elements. These songs later on were sifted and arranged into the four Vedas, which today stand as one of the earliest monuments of ancient literature in the world. These songs were composed in a burst of ecstatic joy on the part of persons who had the gift of composing such verses and for singing these songs. These composers of verses were later on called Ṛṣis, from the word 'Ṛṣ', to see. They were regarded in later times as Ṛṣis or seers of the Vedas or Vedic words, which were considered eternal and indestructible. The theory of the eternity of the Vedas gave needless importance to the arrangement of words, lines, verses and Sūktas or songs. The meanings of these words in course of time were rapidly forgotten; and the sacrificers were fully satisfied with the mere skeleton without the substance. When the songs were composed they were never meant to be used for sacrificers; neither were they taken to be eternal, nor divine. But when we find in later times the frequent use of these mantras in the performance of all kinds of sacrifices, and such words or their combinations regarded as eternal,[1] we cannot but attribute some motive to the guardians of the sacrifices. Was it because the Brāhmaṇas wanted to maintain their superiority over all others in this fashion, or was it because, by making the performance of sacrifices more and more difficult and technical, they wanted to keep off all other kinds of people from attempting to follow their own profession, in much the same way as the primitive sorcerer in an aboriginal tribe tries to maintain his superiority by many an uncanny gesticulation and the handling of many an awe-inspiring object, such as the human skull, human bones, snakes, and so forth, and by his weird incantations?

When orthodox Brāhmaṇism, with its four castes, had grown to be an institution on a more or less permanent basis, it was at once designated as a divine institution,[2] and strict watertight compartments were made of the duties incumbent on each caste. It is not difficult to understand that it was purely with the idea of self-preservation and the preservation of the community that the institution was given out as a divine institution. The natural

[1] This is the chief pivot on which the whole fabric of the Mīmāṁsā philosophy revolves. The Mīmāṁsakas therefore take the greatest pains in establishing the eternity of the Vedic words, and their divinity or अपौरुषेयत्व. cf., for instance, Sāyana, *Ṛgveda Bhāṣya*, Sanskrit Sahitya Parisad Series, No. 9, pp. 36 ff.; also *Jaimini Sūtra*, 1–1–27 and ff., and commentary by Śabara.

[2] cf., for instance, Manu 1–31, where the Brahman creates the four castes from the four different limbs: लोकानां तु विवृध्यर्थं मुखबाहूरुपादः । ब्राह्मणं क्षत्रियं वैश्यं शूद्रं च निरवर्तयत् ॥

consequence of this was the establishment of the theory of Karma, or what is known as act-force. In the physical sphere, we see all acts as pure or impure, good or bad, producing good or bad results. If an offence is committed against the community the offender is punished. Similarly one who has always the good of the community at heart is rewarded. Bad actions were designated sins and good actions merits. But there were many actions which were bad morally, but not so bad as to deserve any punishment or done in a way to escape detection. The question naturally arises as to whether the sin attached to actions of this nature incurs any punishment or not, or whether it can be expiated, and how? The natural consequence of this is the theory of divine punishment or divine rewards. To be logically consistent, a life after death has to be postulated in the theory of transmigration of the soul. The Brāhmaṇas postulated that the body is nothing but a temporary garment within which the soul is contained; and, as a garment becomes in course of time worn out and unfit for use, even so the soul leaves the old decrepit body and seeks new shelters, after having enjoyed the rewards of its good actions in heaven and punishment for bad actions in hell, before returning to earth in a new form. We can thus see how the combined conceptions of the theories of Karma and the transmigration of the soul produced the conceptions of heaven and hell. It is needless to point out that all these theories of Karma, transmigration of the soul, and heaven and hell are not proved by logic or by reason. They were mere speculations to satisfy the curiosity of the primitive mind, to satisfy the vanity of the priestly class, and to preserve society against disruptive forces. The Brāhmaṇas wanted others to take these as divine mandates, wanted the people to regard the authority of the Vedas as absolutely unquestionable, and the existence of God as a matter fully established.

It is in this way that the Brāhmaṇas satisfied themselves and satisfied others by giving a semi-reasonable explanation of as many physical and spiritual phenomena as they could. The final touch was given to this great construction by the theory of emancipation, which proved a deluding mirage to the primitive Aryans and to all who came after them, including scientists, philosophers and magicians. It is extremely difficult to investigate the truth lying behind the conception of emancipation, which has been taken by philosophers of all ages in India as a settled fact. But there is nothing to show that the theory of emancipation was ever proved. The theory of emancipation requires that every individual should undergo a series of births and rebirths till his soul or consciousness is free from all impurities. Emancipation means cessation of births and rebirths, and therefore of worldly miseries. It is this emancipation that every Indian, from the most ancient times up to the present day, strove and strives hard to attain. To the average Indian, therefore, the present life is a misery and devoid of all interests. He cares more for an improved condition in the next birth than his material prosperity in this. The obvious result of this was that emancipation proved to be a philosophy of idleness and apathy towards all things material. Thus the orthodox community went on merrily for several centuries with their favourite social institutions and philosophical speculations, their Vedic mandates and their mystical sacrifices. But later on an unforeseen difficulty arose, when the Vrātyas became sufficiently enlightened and were taken into the orthodox fold in such huge numbers that the Vrātya converts far outnumbered the orthodox members of the society. They were still bolder in their speculations, and seemed to cherish but a scant regard for the 'house of cards' set up by the Brāhmaṇas. India at that time was in a great ferment. Incorporation of the Vrātyas produced a great revolution—a revolution in ideas, speculations, language, dress, customs, manners, and, in fact, everything connected with ancient Indian life. The Vrātyas challenged everything: the caste system, the sacrifices and the Vedas. They formed themselves into many different philosophical schools, and we hear of as many as sixty heretical teachers, each having a peculiar dogma of his own and each having a large number of followers. The materialists were the most bitter opponents of the orthodox Brāhmaṇas. The Brāhmaṇas used to say that the animals immolated in the Jyotiṣṭoma sacrifice went to heaven; the materialists ridiculed them, and said that if the animal immolated in this fashion went to heaven why should not the sacrificer immolate his father whom he was very keen on sending to heaven.[1] When the Brāhmaṇas taught that the present life is nothing and that emancipation is everything, they ridiculed them and said, 'So long as you live, live happily; take much ghee even by running into debt. When the body is reduced to ashes, where is the chance of its coming back to life?'[2] They characterized the authors of the three Vedas as cheats, rogues and night-revellers.[3] The Brāhmaṇas retaliated against them by driving them out of the orthodox community and put a ban on challenging the authority of the Vedas and the Smṛtis, which were a direct outcome of the Vedas. In the *Manusaṁhitā* it is said that if any one of the orthodox community insults the Vedas and the Smrtis by taking recourse to the science of logic, he should be driven out by good men as an atheist and a reviler of the Vedas.[4]

[1] पशुश्चेन्निहतः स्वर्गं ज्योतिष्टोमे गमिष्यति ।
स्वपिता यजमानेन तत्र कस्मान्न हिंस्यते ॥ *Sarva-darśana-saṁgraha*, Bombay Govt. Or. (Hindu) Series, No. I, p. 13.

[2] यावज्जीवेत् सुखं जीवेत् ऋणं कृत्वा घृतं पिबेत् ।
भस्मीभूतस्य देहस्य पुनरागमनं कुतः ॥ op. cit., p. 14.

[3] त्रयो वेदस्य कर्तारो भण्डधूर्तनिशाचराः । op. cit., p. 14.

[4] योऽवमन्येत ते तूभे हेतुशास्त्राश्रयाद्द्विजः ।
स साधुभिर्बहिष्कार्य्यो नास्तिको वेदनिन्दकः ॥ op. cit., II, 11.

CHAPTER II

ORIGIN OF BUDDHIST MAGIC

THE incorporation of the Vrātyas into orthodox society and the growing restlessness of the unincorporated Vrātyas, who already occupied a position of importance by having set up independent kingdoms, produced a great intellectual ferment which shook the very foundation of the orthodox community. The unincorporated Vrātyas often called themselves Kṣattriyas and in this respect they were more or less correct, as they had to lead the life of a warrior as a matter of necessity. Buddha and Mahāvīra, and many other lesser celebrities, were a product of this intellectual ferment. They were the greatest repudiators of orthodoxy and all that it had set up to preserve its cherished institutions. Buddha challenged everything set up by the orthodox community: their caste system, their Vedas, their sacrifices and their philosophical speculations.

It is difficult to determine whether Buddha was a member of the orthodox community. In the traditional books giving an account of the life of Buddha, he is generally mentioned as a Kṣattriya. But he belonged to a place, namely, 'Kapilavāstu', which was quite outside the pale of orthodox influence and surrounded on all sides by territories set up by different Vrātya races. This evidence leads us to think that the family in which Buddha was born was really a Vrātya family, which was erroneously called a Kṣattriya family in olden literature. To be a twice-born in the orthodox sense is to have all the ten sacraments; but in the accounts of the life of Buddha left to us we not only find no mention of all the ten, but also no trace even of the most important sacrament of Upanayana, or the investiture of a sacred thread, which primarily distinguished a Vrātya from an orthodox twice-born. For in the *Manusaṁhitā* we find that if a member of the twice-born caste passed the maximum age-limit prescribed for Upanayana he became a Vrātya, and he obtained a definitely lower status in the community.[1] These considerations point to the fact that Buddha was, in all probability, an unincorporated Vrātya, though later writers considered him to be a Kṣattriya. The fact that Buddha was an unincorporated Vrātya is very important for understanding his teachings, his dogmas and his life-story—inasmuch as his Vrātya-mind and Vrātya-philosophy are traceable in all his undertakings and actions.

If we are to believe in the life-story of Buddha, as recorded, for instance, in the *Lalitavistara*, we have also to believe that Buddha was born of rich parents of the Śākya race ruling in Kapilavāstu. But it has to be pointed out here that the Buddhists themselves do not consider him to be the first founder of the Buddhist religion. They formulate six past Buddhas: Vipaśyī, Śikhī, Viśvabhū, Krakucchanda, Kanakamuni and Kaśyapa, with Gautama Buddha as the seventh, and Maitreya Buddha as the future Buddha, who will come down to earth full 4,000 years after the Mahāparinirvāṇa of Buddha, which is believed to have taken place in the year 483 B.C.

It is not an easy thing to come down to earth and obtain enlightenment, as Buddha did, in one birth; as a matter of fact, the Buddhists formulated that Buddha was born and re-born several hundreds of times, and performed an act of great merit in each of these births. The literature which preserves the life-stories of Buddha is now known as the Jātakas, and there are at least 550 stories of his previous births recorded in the Jātakas. He was

[1] cf. op. cit., II, 39:

अत ऊर्ध्वं त्रयोऽप्येते यथाकालमसंस्कृताः ।
सावित्रीपतिता व्रात्या भवन्त्यार्यविगर्हिताः ॥

born 83 times as a sannyāsin, 58 times as a king, 43 times as a tree-god, 26 times as a preacher, 24 times as a minister, 24 times as a priest, 24 times as an heir-apparent, 23 times as a gentleman, 22 times as a scholar, 20 times as Indra, 18 times as a monkey, 13 times as a merchant, 12 times as a rich man, 12 times as a hen, 10 times as a deer, 10 times as a lion, 8 times as a goose, 6 times as an elephant, 5 times as a Garuḍa, 4 times as a horse, 4 times as a tree, thrice as a potter, thrice as an untouchable, twice as a fish, twice as an elephant-rider, twice as a rat, and once each as a carpenter, ironsmith, frog and hare. In each of these lives Gautama Buddha—the founder of Buddhism—did one or more good deeds of benevolence, renunciation, valour, wisdom, friendship, and charity, and, as a result of good deeds done in innumerable lives in the past, he obtained enlightenment and freedom from the cycle of Saṁsāra.

Siddhārtha,[1] as Gautama Buddha was called in his childhood, was born in the beautiful garden at Lumbinī in the outskirts of the capital city of Kapilavāstu, and his mother died seven days after his birth. Soon after, a Ṛṣi came from the Himalayas, and, after examining the 32 principal and 80 minor characteristics, predicted that if the boy remained a householder he would be a great emperor; but if he renounced the world he would obtain perfect enlightenment. Some time after, Siddhārtha was sent to the house of his preceptor, Viśvāmitra, who was surprised to find that his pupil was proficient in as many as 64 different scripts—more than the preceptor himself knew. The boy quickly mastered the Vedas and Upaniṣads and learnt many other śāstras of the orthodox. He was subsequently brought to the capital and married to Gopā, daughter of Śākya Daṇḍapāṇi. The day the first child was born to him, on that most auspicious day, the young and beautiful Siddhārtha Gautama, prince and heir-apparent

[1] cf. N. J. Krom, *The Life of Buddha*. This account is a summary of the account as preserved in the *Lalitavistara*.

to the throne, renounced the world, alone, unaccompanied, in the search for eternal truth which may bring salvation to mankind. The immediate cause which led to this great renunciation is related in the *Lalitavistara* as follows:

> One day the prince Gautama resolved to visit the gardens in the neighbourhood of his father's city, desiring to examine the beautiful trees and flowers. Then there appeared before his eyes in one of the streets the form of a decrepit old man, his skin shrivelled, his head bald, his teeth gone, his body infirm and bent. A staff supported his tottering limbs, as he stood across the path of the prince's chariot. He asked his charioteer for explanation, and he explained that old age was the common lot of all sentient beings; all that was born must die.
>
> Soon afterwards another strange sight presented itself —a sick man, who was seen tottering on the road, pale and miserable from disease and suffering, scarcely able to draw his breath. The charioteer explained that this was a sick man and that such sickness was common to all.
>
> Soon after, there passed before him a corpse borne on a bier. Siddhārtha asked his charioteer: 'Who is this, borne onwards on his bed, covered with strange garments and surrounded by people weeping and lamenting?' The charioteer said, 'This, my lord, is called a dead body. He has ended his life. He has no further beauty of form, no desires of any kind. He is one with the stone and the fallen tree. He is like a ruined wall or a fallen leaf. No more shall he see his father and mother, brother or sister. His body is dead, and your body must also come to this.'

This was too much for the good prince to bear. He exclaimed:

धिग् यौवनेन जरया समभिद्रुतेन
आरोग्य धिग् विविधव्याधिपराहतेन ।
धिग् जीवितेन पुरुषो न चिरस्थितेन
धिक् पण्डितस्य पुरुषस्य रतिप्रसंगैः ॥

यदि जर न भवेया नैव व्याधिर्न मृत्यु-
स्तथपि च महद्दुःखं पंचस्कन्धं धरन्तो ।
किं पुन ज्वरव्याधिमृत्युनित्यानुबध्दाः
साधु प्रतिनिवर्त्य चिन्तयिष्ये प्रमोचम् ॥[1]

Out upon youth, because old age is running after it. Out upon health, because health is endangered by various diseases. Out upon life, for life is not permanent. Out upon the wise, for they are always seeking for enjoyment. Even if there were no disease, old age and death, the five skandhas will always cause great sufferings. What wonder is there, therefore, if we always have old age, disease and death as our constant companions? Therefore, I must return home and find out the means to relieve the distress of mankind.

Next day, when he was in this mood, he came across a man moving with measured steps, with shaven head and monk's robe, his right shoulder bare, a staff in his right hand and the mendicant's alms-bowl in his left. This man, the charioteer explained, devotes himself to charity and restrains himself, his appetite and bodily desires. He hurts nobody, but does good to all and is full of sympathy for all. The prince asked the man to give an account of himself. The monk said: 'I am called a homeless ascetic. I have forsaken the world, relatives and friends. I seek deliverance of myself and desire the salvation of all creatures and I do harm to none.' The prince forthwith returned to the palace to ask his father's permission to renounce the world. 'I wish to become a wandering ascetic, O father, and to seek Nirvāṇa. All worldly things, O king, are changeable and transitory.' His father was altogether amazed to hear this strange request, and not only did he not grant his request but also kept him under strict surveillance and in very attractive circumstances, so that the young prince's mind might not brood over things spiritual. But the prince possessed so much determination that he renounced the world, leaving his child, his wife, his father and his

[1] *Lalitavistara*, ed. Rajendralal Mitra, p. 230.

relatives, forsaking the riches and pleasures of life and embraced the career of a wandering ascetic. He went from place to place, visiting the well-known philosophers of his time, and studied under them for a considerable length of time; but he did not obtain what he wanted to have. No one could tell him in what lies the salvation of suffering mankind. He was in very great despair, and therefore wanted to take the last recourse to find out the truth—by meditation and introspection and by self-inflicted bodily pain and austerity. He went near Gayā, at Uruvilva, for this purpose, and, with five other ascetics, began the terrible Āsphānaka asceticism, along with its sexennial fast and practice of austerity. Sitting down with his legs folded on a raised seat, exposed to the sun, rain, dew and cold, he reduced his daily ration to one grain of rice, and thus continued for six long years. He was totally exhausted physically and mentally, and at last actually fell unconscious one day. No peace of mind came to him and no divine enlightenment. He became convinced of his folly and took food and nourishment in a natural way, and then the truth dawned on him that freedom from the cycles of countless existences cannot be obtained either by excessive self-mortification or by excessive enjoyments of worldly objects, but only by following a middle course. He meditated further and further, and discovered what is known in Buddhism as the twelve-linked chain of causation. He diagnosed the ultimate cause of worldly miseries as Avidyā, or ignorance, which in a twelve-linked process gives rise to desires. The truth dawned on him that everything in this world is unreal, that everything is non-ego, and that Nirvāṇa is the only calm. He came to know of the four noble truths and the eight-fold noble path which leads to Nirvāṇa. Buddha was determined to teach the doctrines to his fellow-men, and with this purpose in view he went to Mṛgadāva near Benares and preached his doctrine first to his fellow-comrades of Uruvilva, who had deserted him long ago.

This first sermon is called the Dharmacakrapravartana, or the turning of the wheel of the law, as this is the first time Buddha set the wheel of righteousness rolling in the world. Afterwards he moved about throughout upper India converting people to Buddhism, and founded the order of Buddhist monachism. People were admitted into the Saṅgha after they had recited the formula:

बुध्दं शरणं गच्छामि ।
धर्मं शरणं गच्छामि ।
संघं शरणं गच्छामि ।

The Saṅgha was open to all, without distinction of caste and creed, both male and female. Separate monasteries were assigned to monks and nuns; and there were lots of householders as lay-brethren. The success of Buddhism was due to the working out of the idea of establishing a haven of rest to all.

It has already been pointed out that Buddha was a product of a great upheaval, and that he was a great repudiator of Brāhmaṇic orthodoxy. His religion knew no caste bar. He disregarded Sanskrit and preached in the vernacular. He discarded the authority of the Vedas, and God had no place in his religion. His was a religion which knew no mandates and no divine institutions. Yet, nevertheless, Buddha was a product of his particular age, and, therefore, he was not entirely free from the superstitious beliefs current in his time, and the philosophical speculations which were not entirely proved as purely logical conclusions. His religion was based more or less on a fairly rational system. He gave his disciples an opportunity of challenging and examining his doctrines;[1] and never threatened, like the Brāhmaṇas, to outcast those who would challenge the authority of the Vedas and all that was arbitrarily set up by them. Naturally, the Brāhmaṇas and the orthodox community did not encourage Buddha, and regarded him as, more or less, an enemy of orthodoxy. Buddha

[1] He used to say, as we learn from the *Tattvasaṁgraha* (see Foreword, p. clv): परीक्ष्य भिक्षवो ग्राह्यं मद्वचो न तु गौरवात् ।

had naturally to be content with the vast majority of the Vrātyas and the aboriginal inhabitants, who were not raised to the status of the Śūdras probably because of their not getting any opportunity of coming in contact with orthodox Brāhmaṇism. It was perhaps for this reason that he discarded the use of Sanskrit as a medium for his preachings, but employed the vernaculars for the purpose. It was also a remarkable fact that Buddha did not write any comprehensive treatises, embodying his general conclusions and his philosophy. He taught everything orally, and these teachings were collected after his death in a literature which came to be known as the Buddhist Tripiṭaka. When he was living he taught differently to different people with different mentality and a different degree of understanding faculty. It is for this reason that contradictions are sometimes noticeable in his teachings on the same topic.[1]

The theory of transmigration and the consequential chain of births and re-births he took for granted without stopping for a moment to prove it. Similarly, he took emancipation as a settled fact and the theory of Karma in the same way. He believed in the easier method of salvation by the practice of austerities, asceticism and meditation. He carefully incorporated them into his new religious system and preached them to his people. In his time people were steeped in absurd superstitions, and invariably sought to have short-cuts to salvation by easy methods—by the practice of mantras, the practice of self-mortification, and by various other practices, some of which were filthy and revolting.[2] We have conclusive evidence that recourse to mantras was widely taken, as they were believed to bestow magical powers to the individuals

[1] A long discussion on the character of Pudgala as recorded in the *Tattvasaṁgraha*, śl. 348, 349, is an instance in point.

[2] For instance, the practices of the Kāpālikas, a reference to whom has been made in the *Arthaśāstra* of Vṛhaspati, who is undoubtedly earlier than Kauṭilya. See also S.B.E., Vol. XX, p. 89 f.

practising them. Buddha, as a clever organizer, could not fail to notice this type of mentality amongst the masses, which were his favourite field of action, and he did not venture to forbid magical practices altogether in his religion, though it is difficult to say whether he ever believed in their efficacy.[1] Moreover, to make his religion perfect, the founder has not only to take into account the mentality of the intelligentsia by giving them hopes for the next birth and far-off salvation, but also of those who have no conception of distant emancipation, or merits to be gained in the next birth, but are eager to attain worldly prosperities in this very birth.[2] It was to satisfy this second class of the laity that Buddha had to incorporate some sort of mantras, Dhāraṇīs, Mudrās and Maṇḍalas, so that those that might wish to have prosperity in the present birth would feel satisfied[3] by practising them.

In the *Brahmajāla Sūtta*[4] we find mention of a large number of Vidyās or esoteric sciences, which were current in the time of Buddha and condemned by him as *tiracchāna*, or crooked. It is, therefore, easy to conceive that there were many more Vidyās current in his time which were not, in the opinion of Buddha, *tiracchāna*, or crooked, but free from all blame, and these he must

[1] In the *Dīghanikāya* Buddha is represented as saying, 'It is because I see danger in the practice of these mystic wonders that I loathe and abhor and am ashamed thereof' (T. W. Rhys Davids's *Pali English Dictionary*, p. 121). See also the enumeration of the ten kinds of Iddhis, ibid.

[2] cf. *Tattvasaṁgraha*, śl. 3486:

यतोऽभ्युदयनिष्पत्तिर्यतो निःश्रेयसस्य च ।
स धर्म उच्यते तादृक् सर्वैरेव विचक्षणैः ॥

[3] *Tattvasaṁgraha*, śl. 3487:

तदुक्तमन्त्रयोगादिनियमाद्विधिवत् कृतात् ।
प्रज्ञारोग्यविभुत्वादिदृष्टधर्मोऽपि जायते ॥

[4] P.T.S. ed., pp. 9 ff.

have incorporated into his religion. In the *Mañjuśrīmūlakalpa*,[1] which formed part of the extensive Vaipulyasūtra literature of the Buddhists and was probably composed in the first century of the Christian era, we find quite an astonishing number of mantras, Mudrās, Maṇḍalas and Dhāraṇīs, which must have taken their origin in the early centuries B.C., and probably from the time of Buddha himself. Later on, in the *Guhyasamāja*,[2] which is considered as the first systematic Tāntric work of the Buddhists, and which was probably written in the third or the fourth century A.D., we find Buddha saying to the congregation of the faithful, that as the people were not sufficiently enlightened he did not preach the Tāntric system when he was born as the Dīpaṅkara and Kaśyapa Buddha. In the *Sādhanamālā*, a Tāntric work containing about 312 small works called Sādhanas, composed by distinguished writers of the third to the twelfth centuries A.D., we find mention of a fairly large number of mantras originating from Buddha himself.[3] Is there, therefore, any room to doubt that the Tantras and mantras, Mudrās and Dhāraṇīs, were taught by Buddha himself to the lay-brethren who believed in their efficacy? From the Pali literature it can be easily proved that Buddha believed in the doctrine of Iddhis, or supernatural powers, and he mentioned four Iddhipādas: Chhando (will), Viriyam (effort), Cittam (thought), and Vimaṁsā (investigation), which were conducive to the production of superhuman powers.[4]

In the *Vinaya Piṭaka* are recorded two stories which at once show the popularity of the cultivation of magical powers amongst Buddha's own disciples. One is the story of Bhāradvāja, and the other the story of a lay-householder, all of whose relatives

[1] Published in three volumes in the Trivandrum Sanskrit Series.

[2] The work is now published as No. LIII in the Gaekwad's Oriental Series.

[3] See infra, chap. VII.

[4] R. C. Childers, *Dictionary of the Pali Language*, p. 157.

knew how to perform many miracles. Below is given a summary of these two stories from the *Vinaya Piṭaka*, as they have a direct bearing on the subject-matter of this particular chapter.

I. [1]At one time the Seṭṭhi of Rājagṛha had acquired a block of sandalwood of precious flavour. He had a bowl carved out of it, put the same in a balance and had it lifted to the top of a bamboo, which was tied at the top of a succession of bamboos, and publicly declared: 'If any Brāhmaṇa or Śramaṇa be an Arhat and possessed of Iddhi, let him take down the bowl. It is a gift to him.'

Purṇa Kassapa went to the Seṭṭhi and wanted to have the bowl, but the Seṭṭhi asked him to take down the bowl by his miraculous power. Then there came successively Maṅkhāli Gosālā, Ajita Keśakambalī, Pakuda Kaccāyana, Sañjaya Belaṭṭhiputta, and Nigganṭha Ñātaputta, all of whom proffered the same request and received the same reply from the Seṭṭhi.

One morning it so happened that Mahā Moggalāna and Piṇḍola Bhāradvāja were out for alms in the streets of Rājagṛha. Bhāradvāja asked Moggalāna to fetch down the bowl, but as the latter in his turn requested Bhāradvāja to do the same thing, Bhāradvāja, rising up in the air, took the bowl and went thrice round Rājagṛha in the air.

Directly the people came to know of this wonderful feat of miraculous power, they began following in the steps of Bhāradvāja with shouts loud and long. The Blessed One then heard the whole story, and rebuked Bhāradvāja for wantonly displaying his miraculous power before the public for a miserable wooden pot. The Buddha then ruled that whoever should display his superhuman powers before the laity should be guilty of Dukkaṭa, and that whoever should use wooden bowls should be guilty of Dukkaṭa.

[1] S.B.E., Vol. XX, p. 78 f.

II. The second story[1] related to the miraculous powers of the whole family of a layman. In the Bhaddiyanagara there was a householder named Meṇḍaka who, when he had bathed his head, could fill the empty granary by making showers of grain fall from the sky.

When his wife sat down beside a pint pot and vessel for curry and sauce, she could serve the serving men with food: and so long as she did not get up it was not exhausted.

Their son could take up a bag containing a thousand coins, and give to each serving man six months' wages: and so long as as he held it in his hand it was not exhausted.

When their daughter-in-law sat down beside a four-bushel basket, she could give six months' rice to serving men: and so long as she did not get up, it was not exhausted.

When their slave ploughed the land with one ploughshare, seven furrows were formed on the ground.

The Magadha king Seniya Bimbisāra came to know about the miraculous powers of the householder, and wanted to know the whole truth about it. He called his minister and asked him personally to go to the Bhaddiyanagara to test the truth of the rumours. The minister accordingly went to the house of Meṇḍaka and asked him to show his special powers and those of the members of his family. Meṇḍaka showed the identical feats mentioned before, and satisfied the minister and King Bimbisāra about the truth of his miraculous powers.

[1] *Vinaya Piṭaka*, S.B.E., 'Mahāvagga', VI, 34-1-2.

CHAPTER III

GROWTH OF BUDDHIST MAGIC

IN the previous chapter an account has been given of the state of Buddhist magic, when it was in a more or less embryonic condition. In the present chapter an attempt will be made to show how the rudimentary form of magic in Buddhism developed in later times owing to a variety of favourable conditions. These conditions comprise the enforcement of strict discipline among the monks, the gradual changes in the conception of emancipation in the different schools of Buddhism, the enormous growth of Buddhist literature, the introduction of the altruistic philosophy of Mahāyāna—all these factors, though sublime by nature, exercised a great influence on the masses and produced most baneful results which were quite unexpected. It would be reasonably expected that the sublime Mahāyāna philosophy would lead the people to happiness, prosperity and salvation; but, instead, it led them to evil and culminated in Tāntrism, which may justly be called a full-fledged esoteric system.

It will be remembered that from the very start of early Buddhism till the time when Mahāyānism sprang up with all its brilliance, a very strict discipline was enjoined on the followers of the faith. For the Bhikṣus and the Bhikṣuṇīs, who were provided with a haven of rest in the shape of monasteries, the rules were strictly put into operation. Men and women were very strictly kept apart; they were never allowed to have any contact with each other. Men were enjoined to take a vow of celibacy, and the women were asked either not to marry or to abandon their husbands, relatives and children, if there were any. All kinds of luxuries were forbidden, and various foods for which man has a natural desire were entirely tabooed. Wine, fish, meat, appetisers, and many similar objects of enjoyment were specially forbidden. The rules were indeed good, and were very attractive in the time of Buddha, but as they were very unnatural his followers could be expected to follow them only for a certain time, but not for centuries afterwards. It was wholly absurd to expect obedience to such strict disciplinary measures from all members of the Saṅgha even in Buddha's lifetime, to say nothing of centuries after his Mahāparinirvāṇa. Buddha's was a great personality, and so long as he was alive the majority of his followers dared not commit any offence by going against his wishes.

But all were not of the same mentality; there were monks in his own time who used to send, contrary to his specific injunctions, wreaths of flowers to wives, daughters, young women and female slaves, to sit on one seat, lie on one bed, one mat, one coverlet, with the wives and daughters and young women and female slaves, to eat food at any time, to drink strong drinks, to dance, to sing and play music, and all these together in every combination. These monks must have considered in their minds what the result would be by forgoing all the pleasures of life, by strictly following the injunctions imposed on the Saṅgha by Buddha. The promise of freedom from births and rebirths may be only a possibility, and success at best is very questionable. This particular set of monks, therefore, instead of running after a deluding Nirvāṇa, violated the rules of discipline and took to worldly enjoyments. Buddha was very much perturbed when he heard of the infamous conduct of his followers, and sent some of his trusted disciples to carry out his order of expulsion from the Saṅgha against these monks.[1]

Thus the members of the Saṅgha must have revolted from time to time against the unnatural rules of discipline, and party quarrels on such points were already in evidence in the second

[1] S.B.E., Vol. XVII, p. 347 f.

great council, when the Mahasāṅghikas were expelled from the church by the Sthaviras because the latter were unwilling to make any concessions on the ten minor points of discipline raised by the youngsters. Rebellion against the rules on broader and more important matters of discipline must have been in existence among the monks; but they could not create a party of their own which would be able to cope sufficiently with the orthodox section, which was sure to go against them and denounce them as heretics. Those monks, who saw salvation only from leading a natural life and did not like to forgo the pleasures of the world, went on devising plans in secret, and probably writing what are called the original Tantras, which were secretly handed down through successive chains of preceptors and disciples who could practise the rites only in secret. These Tantras are in the form of Saṅgītis,[1] and are said to have been delivered by Buddha in an assembly of the faithful. It is in this Saṅgīti form that all new ideas, dogmas and philosophical speculations were introduced into Buddhism, and the Saṅgītis, we must remember, were very powerful agencies in the introduction of innovations.

The orthodox followers of the faith were sure to challenge anything that was not said by Buddha. That seems to be the reason of the great popularity of the Saṅgīti literature. The original Tantras of Buddhism were therefore, in the Saṅgīti form, wherein were inculcated doctrines which were diametrically opposed to the teachings of Buddha. Easy methods leading to happiness in this world were held out in this literature. Easy paths leading to salvation were shown. Great parade was made of the merits to be gained by the repetition of the mantras, Dhāraṇīs, and panegyrics, and by the worship of innumerable gods and goddesses. But everywhere any casual reader can

[1] The Saṅgītis begin with एवं मया श्रुतमेकस्मिन् भगवान् . . . विहरति स्म । In this literature Buddha is introduced in an Assembly of the Faithful, where he is represented as delivering sermons on diverse points of Dharma.

detect a desire on the part of the authors to thwart all unnatural rules and regulations forcibly chained on to the followers of Buddhism. These disciplinary regulations were gradually relaxed one after another, and ultimately, when the Vajrayānists gained in power and got an overwhelming majority, a general revolution was declared against the orthodox Mahāyāna, which in course of time dwindled to nothingness, as it was powerless to fight the growing disorder amongst the Tāntrics.

It is thus quite clear that there was nothing inherently wrong when Buddha imposed certain moral discipline on his disciples. On the contrary, they were very attractive in his time. People praised them and Buddha got a large number of converts. It is a most tragic event in the history of the subsequent development of Buddhism, that the strictness of discipline actuated a large section of Buddhists in later times to revolt against it and undo everything that the founder of the religion had attempted to accomplish, and bring about a disgraceful degeneration in Buddhism and weaken its very foundations. But how this degeneration helped the growth of Buddhist magic will be shown in the sequel.

There was another disturbing factor which helped the degeneration of Buddhism, though the factor itself was quite lofty and laudable. This was the development of the idea of Buddhist emancipation, or Nirvāṇa, as it was termed by Buddha. Buddha was himself satisfied when the truth of Nirvāṇa dawned on him: this was a loftier doctrine than any the leading Sāṅkhya philosophers of his age taught. But did he define Nirvāṇa? No. Whenever questioned, his usual answer was: 'You should first realize Nirvāṇa and then you can know what it is. You need not know that even. The attainment of Nirvāṇa will give you freedom from births and rebirths, which means emancipation.' In the first century B.C., in the *Milinda Pañho*,[1] we

[1] *The Questions of King Milinda*, S.B.E., Part II, pp. 186 ff., 'Dilemma the Eighth. The Outward Form of Nirvāṇa.'

find a glowing account of Nirvāṇa. But there also we do not meet with a reference to the condition of the individual when he attains Nirvāṇa. In the first century A.D., Aśvaghoṣa, in his *Saundarananda*,[1] compares Nirvāṇa to the extinction of a flame—as a lamp goes out when the oil is exhausted, even so the individual is extinguished when there is no more suffering, or Kleśa, to his credit. This is practically the last word of the Hīnayānic interpretation of Nirvāṇa. With the Mahāyānists the interpretation became different. They were not satisfied with the mystic silence of Buddha on the most important philosophical concept promised to the followers as a reward for all the moral restrictions practised by them in this life. They wanted to speculate, and formulated that Nirvāṇa is nothing but Śūnya, which meant, according to the Madhyamaka conception, a condition about which neither existence nor non-existence, nor a combination of the two, nor a negation of the two, can be predicated.[2] This is the theory of the great Nāgārjuna—the founder of the Madhyamaka system of Buddhist philosophy, who flourished in the second century A.D.[3]

But can this Śūnya, as defined by Nāgārjuna, satisfy anybody, even intellectual men, not to speak of the ignorant masses? It is a condition similar to a transcendental condition, and, in fact, much worse truth than the mystic silence of Buddha.

The Yogācāras, therefore, came to their rescue. They retained the term 'Śūnya'; but formulated that it was not an empty Śūnya, as proposed by the Madhyamakas, but a positive Śūnya with a positive element of Vijñāna.[4] People heaved a sigh of relief. On the attainment of Nirvāṇa, therefore, the individual

[1] Ed. Mm. Haraprasād Śāstrī, in the *Bibliotheca Indica*, p. 102, XVI, 28, 29.

[2] cf. *Sarvadarśanasaṁgraha*, p. 23: अस्तिनास्तितदुभयानुभयचतुष्कोटिविनिर्मुक्तं शून्यरूपम् । Also *Advayavajrasaṁgraha*, p. 19, ll. 21–22, G.O.S., No. XL.

[3] Nāgārjuna also explained Nirvāṇa by six negatives. cf. *Madhyamaka Kārikā*, chap. XXV, Kārikā, 3.

[4] Yamakami Sogen, *Systems of Buddhist Thought*, chap. VI.

neither attains complete extinction, nor does he go out like a lamp, nor pass into a condition which cannot be conceived. The Yogācāra idea of emancipation satisfied the people for a time. It is believed that Maitreya was the author of the Yogācāra school of thought.

Soon after, a time came when Vijñānavāda also could not satisfy all. Some greater brains came forward with a new doctrine and introduced it into the conception of Yogācāra. This new introduction was known as the Mahāsukhavāda,[1] and the form of Buddhism which was based on this Mahāsukhavāda was known as Vajrayāna, or the adamant-vehicle. In Vajrayāna Nirvāṇa had three elements: 'Śūnya, Vijñāna and Mahāsukha.' This triple combination of Śūnya was termed by them as Vajra; because, as they said, it is firm and sound, unchangeable, unpierceable, impenetrable, incombustible and indestructible.[2] They formulated that Śūnya is Nirātmā, and a goddess in whose eternal embrace the individual mind, i.e. the Bodhicitta, or Vijñāna, is locked, and there remains in eternal bliss and happiness.

It was no fault of original Buddhism that its conception of Nirvāṇa should take so many shapes and culminate in Mahāsukhavāda, which would considerably weaken the religion and plunge Buddhism headlong into the deepest abyss of degeneration.

The third factor which, though sublime in its conception, brought about degeneration, is the evolution of the idea of Karuṇā. It must be remembered that Buddha advised his followers to obtain Nirvāṇa for themselves by their own efforts. They should have nothing to do with others or their sufferings or miseries. It

[1] The character of Mahāsukha is described in the *Jñānasiddhi*, chap. VII. See *Two Vajrayāna Works*, G.O.S., No. XLIV, p. 57. Also *Advayavajrasaṁgraha*, G.O.S., No. XL, intro., p. xxxviii, and p. 50.

[2] दृढं सारमसौशीर्यं अच्छेद्याभेद्यलक्षणम् । अदाहि अविनाशि च शून्यता वज्रमुच्यते ॥ Quoted from the *Yogaratnamālā* in the *Bauddha Gān O Dohā*, p. 8; also from *Vajraśekhara* in the *Advayavajrasaṁgraha*, op. cit., p. 23, 11, 23–4.

was different when Mahāyānism came forth later on, with its dazzling conception of Karuṇā, or compassion, for all human beings. They designated themselves as Mahāyānists, and denounced the self-seeking monks of the old style as Hīnayānists. The Mahāyānists differed from the Hīnayānists on several important points, though for both of them the realization of Nirvāṇa, which leads to the cessation of sufferings, was imperative. But the methods followed by the two branches of Buddhism were widely different, if not altogether antagonistic. The Hīnayānists obtain Nirvāṇa, or the freedom from suffering and the consequential repetition of births and rebirths, or virtually an extinction of self altogether. But it must be remembered that, even if they are able to gain Nirvāṇa, they cannot realize the perfect truth or remove the veil which conceals the transcendental truth; nor can they impart the knowledge of salvation to others. The Mahāyānists, on the other hand, do not care for their own salvation; they are more solicitous about the deliverance of their fellow-creatures, who are in the grip of constant suffering, than about their own. They are not afraid of Saṁsāra, or the cycle of births and rebirths, in the same sense as the Hīnayānists are; but they are always ready to undergo any troubles and sufferings, if these lead even in a small measure to the spiritual uplift of their fellow beings. Their compassion for suffering humanity actuates them to renounce their merits or even their salvation, and as a reward for this selfless sacrifice they are able to remove the veil covering the transcendental truth, and become omniscient.[1] This ideal of a Mahāyānist finds expression in the *Kāraṇḍavyūha*,[2] where the example of Avalokiteśvara—the

[1] *Tattvasaṁgraha* of Śāntarakṣita, G.O.S., Nos. XXX, XXXI, pp. 869, 870, 872. Also B. Bhattacharyya, foreword to the above work, pp. xlvii ff.

[2] Satyavrata Sāmāśramī's ed., Calcutta, p. 21:

या(ता ?)वदवलोकितेश्वरस्य बोधिसत्वस्य दृढप्रतिज्ञा न परिपूरिता भवन्ति सर्वसत्वाः सर्वदुःखेभ्यः प रिमोक्षिता यावदनुत्तराया:(यां ?) सम्यक्सम्बोधौ न प्रतिष्ठापिता भवन्ति ॥

all-compassionate Bodhisattva—is set up, who refused his salvation, though fully entitled to it, until all creatures of the world were in possession of the Bodhi knowledge and obtained freedom from worldly miseries.

It is said that when Avalokiteśvara Bodhisattva,[1] after obtaining Nirvāṇa, was about to merge himself in the eternal Śūnya from the summit of the Sumeru mountain he heard an uproar from a very remote quarter and became remorseful. He sat there forthwith in intense meditation, and immediately realized that the uproar was nothing but the wailings of the people at the disappearance of Avalokiteśvara, the all-compassionate Bodhisattva. In their utter helplessness at the prospect of losing the support of Avalokiteśvara, who was their only saviour from their worldly miseries and sufferings, they rent the skies with their bitter wailings. Avalokiteśvara was deeply moved when he came to know about this, and resolved within himself not to accept his well-merited emancipation so long as even a single individual on earth remained unemancipated. In the *Kāraṇḍavyūha* we hear him saying that he will live and act for the uplift of humanity till the end of creation before merging himself in Śūnya. He will take the form of Viṣṇu and impart lessons in Dharma to those who worship him; he will take the form of Śiva in order to impart lessons to those who worship him; he will take the form of Gaṇeśa and impart lessons to those who worship him; he will take the form of a king in order to impart lessons to those who admire and love their king; he will even take the forms of father and mother, in order to teach Dharma to those who worship them.[2] This theory of Karuṇā was an outstanding feature in the

[1] For an account of Avalokiteśvara see the notice of the MS. *Guṇakāraṇḍavyūha*, in Rajendralal Mitra's *Sanskrit Buddhist Literature of Nepal*, p. 95.

[2] *Kāraṇḍavyūha*, op. cit., pp. 21–22; also B. Bhattacharyya, *Indian Buddhist Iconography*, pp. 32 ff.

Mahāyāna religion, and such a high ideal as Avalokiteśvara's is unprecedented in the history of any other religion of the world. It was no fault of Buddhism that, though it set up such a high ideal, the result was most disappointing. Buddhism, we should remember, both in its earlier and later stages of development, was mostly concerned with the masses and people of low castes with lower degrees of intellectual development. The high ideal of Karuṇā was too much for them; but every individual follower of the faith had to associate himself with the theory of Karuṇā in some way or other. Day after day, without realizing its importance, they had to resolve that they would devote all their energies and sacrifice everything dear to them for the uplift of humanity. Day after day, they had to repeat this pious wish, till after a time it became a mere convention entirely bereft of its import and importance; and, what is worse, the priests found in this theory of Karuṇā an excuse for the grossest forms of immorality and lawlessness.[1]

In the course of time, the literature of the Buddhists of both the Hīnayāna and Mahāyāna schools had developed to such an enormous extent that it had become almost impossible to give any benefit from this literature to the lay-brethren, whose intellectual faculties were mostly far below the ordinary. The priests held that the perusal of the Buddhist literature was capable of conferring great merits on the followers of the faith. The perusal and the handling of lengthy works were found difficult even for those who possessed some intellectual superiority. It was in response to popular demands that the priests had to shorten the books to suit popular needs. Take, for example, *Aṣṭasāhasrikāprajñāpāramitā*, which is a fairly stupendous

[1] cf. *Chittaśodhanaprakaraṇa*, in J.A.S.B., LXVII, p. 178:

बोधिचित्तं समुत्पाद्य सम्बोधौ कृतचेतसा ।
तन्नास्ति यन्न कर्तव्यं जगदुद्धरणाशयैः ॥

and difficult work for a tolerably learned Buddhist to read through and understand. It was therefore shortened into the form of *Śataślokī Prajñāpāramitā*, in one hundred stanzas; and the people were asked to read and memorize it. For many this, too, proved very trying, and it was soon reduced to a *Prajñāpāramitāhṛdayasūtra*—a still shorter form. This was further shortened into a *Prajñāpāramitā Dhāraṇī*, in a few unintelligible words, and this ultimately gave rise to the mantra of Prajñāpāramitā. It was given out to the people that if either the mantra, the Dhāraṇī, the Hṛdaya Sūtra or the longer forms of the work were once recited, the merit to be gained by a perusal of the complete Prajñāpāramitā was obtainable. In Tibet they made the process still shorter and easier. They prepared prayer-wheels, in which were contained their favourite books, soldered up the covers, and went on turning the wheels round and round. Their belief was that by each turn of the wheel the worshipper gained the merit of perusing the entire literature contained in the wheel.

What wonder is it that Buddhism should degenerate under these unfavourable circumstances, and people should grow more superstitious by running after easier and cheaper methods for obtaining salvation!

CHAPTER IV

RISE OF VAJRAYĀNA

IT has been seen how primitive Buddhism, as taught by Buddha, passed through many changes and underwent degeneration owing to a variety of circumstances which cropped up in later times. This degenerated form of Buddhism is what is called Vajrayāna, or Tāntric Buddhism. We have already mentioned that Buddhism was a challenge to, and a repudiation of, earlier Brāhmaṇism. It was now the part of Tāntric Buddhism to challenge the authority of Buddha and repudiate the original Buddhism.

Buddha enforced a large number of unnatural and strict rules for the guidance of his followers. All kinds of worldly enjoyments were forbidden, especially wine, women, fish, meat and all kinds of exciting food. All these the Tāntrics of the later age introduced into their religion in the form of five Makāras, and they did so with a vengeance, and even went so far as to declare that without these emancipation was impossible.

With regard to Buddha, they said that he was only an ordinary mortal Buddha, and it was through him that the eternal truth of Buddhism came to the world. Truth is the all-important factor in Buddhism. Buddha served only as a post-office, as many other Buddhas had done previously and will do in future. Thus Buddha lost his importance in the religion founded and preached by him. They formulated the theory of the five Dhyāni Buddhas,[1] each with a Śakti attached to him, as presiding over the

[1] This theory was for the first time formulated in the *Guhyasamāja*, first chapter, now published in the Gaekwad's Oriental Series.

five Skandhas, or elements.[1] These Dhyāni Buddhas are a peculiar class of Buddhas, who are eternal and have not to pass through the lower stages of the Bodhisattva.[2] The Dhyāni Buddha and the Śakti bring forth a number of Bodhisattvas, who look after creation. Under the regime of each Bodhisattva eight mortal Buddhas are required to appear in the world, to preach the doctrines and help the people to emancipate themselves. From this, the position occupied by Buddha in later days can be easily comprehended.

Then there is the theory of emancipation. Buddha did not like to define Nirvāṇa, and whenever questioned on this point he remained silent. The Tāntrics defined Nirvāṇa as Śūnya, Vijñāna and Mahāsukha, and explained the condition of the Bodhi-mind in Nirvāṇa as in the embrace of a woman. The Tāntrics associated themselves with a number of women, whom they designated as Śaktis, and their union was termed Yoga, which they said was a powerful agency for the attainment of salvation. In the earlier Buddhism instructions were given to individuals to attain Nirvāṇa. The Nirvāṇa was entirely narrow in its outlook, which made the priests self-seeking and regardless of the sufferings of their fellow creatures. The theory of Karuṇā was a direct challenge to this form of Nirvāṇa. But the Tāntrics, who were leading lives of great sin and immorality, found in the theory of Karuṇā, or self-sacrifice, an excuse for their heinous doings. The Bodhisattva, they stated, is daily making untold sacrifices for suffering humanity, and, therefore, there is nothing that he should not do,[3] meaning thereby that the theory of Karuṇā gives him a blank charter for committing all kinds of heinous offences and violating all laws, human or divine. They formulated the theory that

[1] cf. *Jñānasiddhi*, op. cit.:

पञ्चबुध्दस्वभावत्वात् पञ्चस्कन्धा जिनाः स्मृताः

[2] Kern, *Manual of Indian Buddhism*, p. 64.

[3] J.A.S.B., Vol. LXVII, p. 178: तन्नास्ति यन्न कर्तव्यं जगदुध्दरणाशयैः ।

these three worlds have been created by the Holder of the Thunderbolt for the enjoyment and benefit of the worshippers.[1] They further said that one who strives after salvation should always enjoy Prajñāpāramitā, or the perfect truth. This Prajñā, they said, resides in every woman on earth, and they should be enjoyed without reservation. Good, bad, indifferent, diseased and depraved, all are welcome to him. No distinction should be made between women of higher castes or lower castes, and no women, even those closely related, should be allowed to escape.[2] Their favourite slogan was:

कर्मणा येन वै सत्त्वा: कल्पकोटिशतान्यपि ।
पच्यन्ते नरके घोरे तेन योगी विमुच्यते ॥

> By those identical actions by which mortals rot in hell for hundreds of crores of cycles, the Yogin is liberated.[3]

The Tāntrics had many things which, when brought to public notice, were likely to give a rude shock to the people at large. In other words, secrecy was their keynote in the beginning, till the practices enjoined in the Tantras were widely current. In the *Guhyasamāja* there are many practices which cannot be made public until the ground is prepared to receive them. Thus the Tantra went into private hands, and was transmitted in the most secret manner possible through an unbroken chain of gurus and disciples, till it gained currency after about 300 years,[4] mainly through the teachings and mystic songs of the 84 Siddhapuruṣas and their disciples, and all those who came into intimate contact with them. These Mahāsiddhas mostly belonged to the seventh,

[1] *Prajñopāyaviniścayasiddhi*, in *Two Vajrayāna Works*, G.O.S., No. XLIV, p. 23, verse 31.

[2] *Prajñopāyaviniścayasiddhi*, op. cit., p. 22 f., verses 22, 23 ff.

[3] *Jñānasiddhi*, op. cit., p. 31, śl. 15.

[4] This appears evident from a statement in *Tārānātha* referred to by Kern in his *Manual of Indian Buddhism*, p. 133. *Tārānātha*, p. 201.

eighth and ninth centuries of the Christian Era,[1] at a time when Vajrayāna had already made great headway and was almost casting into the shade the original and the purer form of the Buddhist religion. They wrote in a language which was designated by them as the Sandhyābhāṣā, or the twilight language, meaning thereby that the contents may be explained either by the light of day or by the darkness of night. The songs composed by the Mahāsiddhas were all written in this language, which had always a hidden or a mystic meaning.

It has been made abundantly clear that Vajrayāna was a direct development of the Yogācāra philosophy of Mahāyāna Buddhism, which was started by Maitreyanātha in the third century A.D. According to Yogācāra, the world, as we see it, has no existence. It is the creation of the mind or the momentary consciousness which is real. The worldly phenomena, according to Yogācāra, are like a dream or as if set up by magic. All individuals are composed of a chain of momentary consciousness, which passes through a series of births and rebirths until it is emancipated, when births and rebirths cease. The realization of Śūnya, they said, leads to the attainment of omniscience, or the quality of knowing all things. They formulated that there are two kinds of obstructions,[2] which, when destroyed by the realization of the voidness of the universe, lead to the attainment of omniscience. The first is called the Kleśāvaraṇa, or the obstruction of sufferings, and the second is the Jñeyāvaraṇa, or the obstruction hiding the transcendental truth. Sufferings are feelings such as attachment, antipathy, etc., which are indeed hindrances to knowing a thing as it is. The other obstruction is the want of perfect knowledge or the highest truth, and the inability to impart that true knowledge to others for their benefit. The first kind of veil or obstruction can be removed only by the realization of the voidness of the

[1] See infra, chap. VIII.

[2] Foreword to *Tattvasaṁgraha*, op. cit., p. xlvii.

universe. The feelings of attachment, hatred, etc., indeed result in the first kind of obstruction; and these impure feelings are caused not by external objects, but by the constant practice of thinking of the Ego as real. The realization of Nairātmya destroys the Ego and its connexion with the surrounding objects, which are unreal, as also the feelings of attachment, antipathy, etc., which are only the outcome of thinking the Ego real. The constant meditation on Nairātmya removes the veil and the ascetic is then, after considerable practice, able to discover that everything is void. This kind of intense meditation leads to the realization of Nairātmya of the universe in a way very similar to a man's perception of a lovely damsel about whom he is constantly thinking and keenly meditating. If constant thinking about the Ego and its connexion with the objective world is once destroyed by the realization of Nairātmya, it will not possibly again come up in that chain of Vijñāna or consciousness. The Śrāvakas and Pratyekas, who are mortally afraid of the cycle of existence and desire emancipation only for the self, stand always in need of this kind of meditation for extinction of the Ego altogether from their chain of Vijñāna. The Mahāyānists, who, on the other hand, were imbued with their unbounded feelings of compassion for suffering humanity and who were always prepared to help all beings troubled with great suffering, were induced by their feeling of compassion to practise this kind of meditation for the realization of Nairātmya. But between the Hīnayānist and the Mahāyānist there is only this difference—that, while the Hīnayānist is selfish, the Mahāyānist is selfless in the matter of removing the first kind of veil by meditation on the Nairātmya of the external world.

The second kind of obstruction, namely, the veil covering the transcendental truth, can only be removed by constant meditation on Nairātmya with great reverence and without cessation. By meditating thus the veil is removed and the ascetic becomes omniscient; and in this lies the most fundamental difference between the Hīnayāna and Mahāyāna. Though the Śrāvakas and Pratyekas are able to realize Nairātmya, they cannot obtain omniscience, because of their inability to identify themselves with the universe as the Mahāyānists are able to do from their unbounded compassion for suffering humanity. The Hīnayāna, or the lower vehicle, therefore, is an easier path leading to salvation, but the Mahāyāna, or the greater vehicle, is much more difficult inasmuch as it involves a great self-sacrifice without the prospect of obtaining any reward. For even when, by the removal of the veil of Jñeyāvaraṇa, omniscience is attained, they are required to employ all their religious merit for the uplift of suffering humanity and until all creatures of the world obtain salvation. With the deliverance of the world and with the emancipation of the inmates of Saṁsāra, all Bodhisattvas may enter Nirvāṇa and be emancipated.

In order to define more clearly certain principal tenets, it is proposed to give here a succinct summary of a highly technical Vajrayāna work, entitled the *Prajñopāyaviniścayasiddhi*,[1] composed by Anaṅgavajra, one of the 84 Siddhācāryas, who flourished at about the end of the seventh century A.D. In the first chapter the author defines Bhava, or existence, which originates from false reflections, or the reflection (Kalpanā) of the worldly phenomena as real. Existence gives rise to manifold sufferings and to a large number of actions and their results. From them originate birth and death and a variety of such sufferings. So long as the people of the universe consider its outward manifestations as really due to ignorance, they neither do good to themselves nor to the people at large. It is for this reason that the followers of Buddhism, who are bent upon emancipating the three worlds, should abandon the reflection of reality. Once reality is abandoned,

[1] Published in the Gaekwad's Oriental Series, under the title *Two Vajrayāna Works.*

one should not go to the other extreme and think of everything as unreal. Granting that there is difference between the two, in the cognition there exists no such difference. It is better to take the world as real rather than to reflect on everything as unreal, because the lamp which is burning can go out; but how can it be extinguished in Nirvāṇa when it is not burning? Reflection of reality should be abandoned, because it is like magic; so also that of unreality, because it is non-existent. When the conception of unreality is abandoned, it gives rise to a state which is neither Saṁsāra nor Nirvāṇa. Realization of the voidness (Śūnyatā) of all worldly phenomena, after careful differentiation between knowledge and the object of knowledge, is what is known as the highest knowledge, or the knowledge of Prajñā. Compassion is of the nature of affection (Rāga), as it removes sufferings (Rañjati) which spring up from numberless causes. Compassion is called Upāya, or means, because it always, like a boat, leads him towards the goal. The commingling of the two—Prajñā and Upāya—is like the commingling of water and milk; in it the duality is merged into one without distinction and is called Prajñopāya. This Prajñopāya is the creative principle of the universe, and everything emerges and develops from this principle. It is called Mahāsukha, because it gives eternal happiness, and is known as Samantabhadra, as it is wholly auspicious.

The second chapter opens with the remark that perfect knowledge cannot be defined, as it is dependent more or less on self-realization, and, therefore, previous teachers have not attempted any definition in the numerous Sūtrāntas, or works on mantras and their practices. Perfect knowledge can only be obtained from a qualified preceptor, and without him, however much one may try, one cannot get it. Thus the worshipper fails to attain success, as a field, though well-tilled, cannot produce if the seed is wanting. It is, therefore, very necessary that a preceptor well-versed in the Tāntric lore should be served and worshipped with great devotion, so that the knowledge may be attained eventually and perfection may be gained. As the Sūryakānta (sun-crystal) jewel burns when it comes in contact with the rays of the sun, so also the Citta (mind) jewel of the disciple suddenly bursts into flames when it comes in contact with the preceptor, who, after having realized the truth, radiates strong rays of knowledge.

The third chapter deals with the initiation of the disciple into Prajñopāya. The preceptor is to be approached by the disciple in the company of the Mahāmudrā (the great woman), who appears charming in outward appearance and is profusely decked in ornaments. Then the disciple worships the preceptor with a long panegyric, and at the end entreats the guru to grant him initiation, so that he may be regarded as belonging to the family (*kula*) of the Buddhas as their offspring. The preceptor, as a mark of great favour, then grants the requisite initiation, after associating the disciple in the presence of the assembly with the Mahāmudrā previously described. Further on, the guru gives him the five Samayas and imparts instructions on Samvara, or restraint, imposed on a Bodhisattva. The initiated disciple thereupon pays his compliments to the preceptor for this act of great kindness, which has given him the much-longed-for freedom from suffering, and takes a solemn vow to place beings in the three worlds in the sphere of Buddha-hood after obtaining it himself.

In the fourth chapter the author dilates on the meditation of Prajñopāya. This consists of the meditation on something which is neither Śūnya nor its opposite, nor a negation of the two. By the acceptance of Śūnya, or Aśūnya, numerous false constructions arise, and in their attempted abandonment the determination to abandon them arises. Therefore both these should be given up. In the attempt to abandon both Śūnyatā and the determination also, the cognition of self becomes predominant. Therefore, all such methods should be given up. The worshipper should think himself as unchanging, absolute, nameless, stainless, without a beginning or an end, like the sky. The compassionate Bodhisattva should not neglect beings in misery, nor should he think whether they exist or not. The Prajñā is so called because it does not admit of transformation, and the Kṛpā (compassion) is so called because it tries to do good to all beings, like the Cintāmaṇi jewel. The Prajñā is absolute; Kṛpā, or compassion, is absolute. They both commingle together in cognition. When this commingling takes place, there is neither the knower, nor the knowledge, nor the object of knowledge; and that is exactly what is called the highest knowledge. There is neither any doer nor enjoyer, because it is free from the knowledge of either the doer or the enjoyer. It is called the knowledge of the great truth. In this there is no receiver, no giver, no object to be given; no object to be taken. Those who have realized this great truth acquire innumerable attainments, even while doing ordinary things such as seeing, hearing, talking, laughing and eating, or when their attention is otherwise diverted. This truth is also known as non-duality, the Bodhi-mind, thunderbolt or Vajrasattva, the enlightened one or the enlightenment. This is also known as Prajñāpāramitā, the embodiment of all Pāramitās, or Samatā or equality, or the best object of meditation for all classes of the Buddhas. In this, the world with its movable and immovable objects, takes its origin, and from this spring forth the innumerable Bodhisattvas, Sambuddhas and Śrāvakas. The ascetic should meditate on this, leaving aside the constructions of reality and non-reality; and whoever is able to cast off reality and non-reality attains perfection quickly. By thus shaking off sins he becomes free from sufferings, and attains countless qualities which are excellent and conduce to enlightenment.

The author then gives us two charming verses describing Saṁsāra and Nirvāṇa, and in fact these two in a great measure point to the height to which Vajrayānists had reached in the matter of transcendental philosophy. Saṁsāra is defined as:

अनल्पसंकल्पतमोऽभिभूतं
प्रभंजनोन्मत्ततडिच्चलं च ।
रागादिदुर्वारमलावलिप्तं
चित्तं हि संसारमुवाच वज्री ॥[1]

The holder of the thunderbolt defines Saṁsāra as the condition of the mind which is overwhelmed with the darkness arising out of numerous false constructions, is as fleeting as the lightning in a storm, and is besmeared with the dirt of attachment, etc., not easily removable.

Nirvāṇa he defines again as a directly opposite condition of the mind:[2]

प्रभास्वरं कल्पनया विमुक्तं
प्रहीणरागादिमलप्रलेपम् ।
ग्राह्यं न च ग्राहकमग्रसत्त्वं
तदेव निर्वाणवरं जगाद ॥[3]

He also said that the excellent Nirvāṇa is another condition of the mind, which is bright with purity, is free from all false constructions and the dirt of attachment, etc., which does not know and cannot be known, and is eternal.

In the fifth chapter practical hints are given to the disciple with regard to certain Tāntric practices, called the Tattvacaryā, for the attainment of salvation. This Tattvacaryā, the author says, is adored even by the greatest Hindu gods like Murāri, Śiva, Indra and Kubera; and by carrying on these practices

[1] op. cit., p. 18, śl. 22.

[2] This definition reminds us of the well-known differentiation made by Nāgārjuna in his *Madhyamaka Kārikā*:

निर्वाणस्य च या कोटिः कोटिः संसरणस्य च ।
न तयोरन्तरं किंचित् सुसूक्ष्ममपि विद्यते ॥

—chap. XXV, Kārikā 20.

[3] op. cit., p. 18, śl. 23.

systematically the Tathāgatas obtained the highest emancipation. The practices consist in the observance of the different rules pointed out in the Mantrayāna, namely the Samayas, the five nectars, partaking the Pradīpa (ordures) and the constant company of women, who are the different forms of Prajñāpāramitā on earth.

The author further on points out that through enjoyment alone the ascetic can attain perfection in one life, provided that his mind is directed towards the Bodhi, and if he is able rightly to perceive the inner nature of the outward phenomena of the world as void, and if he makes ceaseless efforts to relieve the distress of all beings. If the world is realized as nothing but a dream, or as if set up by magic, and if the mind is free from all false reflections and is pure by nature, then it is faced with no obstruction for obtaining the Bodhi. The author concludes by saying that those who look upon profit and loss, honour and insult, misery and happiness, blame and praise with the same eye, who are free from all false constructions, are always compassionate towards worldly beings, and are the followers of the vehicles of the Caryā, obtain Bodhi without any difficulty.

From the foregoing it can be easily seen that Vajrayāna took into account all the best philosophical tenets and theories, and, in fact, incorporated all that was best in Buddhism, and probably in Hinduism also, and it was owing to this fact that it attained great popularity. It satisfied everybody: the cultured and the uncultured, the pious and the habitual sinners, and the lower and the higher ranks of people and devotees. Vajrayāna, which outwardly appeared to be a very demoralizing religion, and went against all the teachings of Buddha and of the great patriarchs of Buddhism, became extremely popular, simply because it was able to cater for all tastes and because it was cosmopolitan in character.

CHAPTER V

THE PLACE OF ORIGIN

IT is difficult to suggest the exact place where Tāntrism originated. The introduction of Śakti worship in religion is so un-Indian that we are constrained to admit it as an external or foreign influence. Some of the Tantras also support this view.[1] But these Tāntrics, who incorporated Śakti worship into their religion, had some strongholds of their own from which the Tantras were disseminated amongst the Indian people and became popular. In the *Sādhanamālā*[2] we find mention of four Pīṭhas, or sacred spots, of the Vajrayānists, namely: Kāmākhyā, Sirihaṭṭa, Pūrṇagiri and Uḍḍiyāna. The identification of the first two is certain. Both are situated in the province of Assam. Kāmākhyā is now known as Kāmākhyā or Kāmarūpa, which is only a few miles distant from Gauhati, the capital of Assam. Sirihaṭṭa is the modern Sylhet. But the identification of the two others has given rise to much speculation and theorising. Pūrṇagiri is sometimes identified with the modern Poona; but this is very doubtful, though at this stage it is extremely difficult to suggest any identification.[3] Uḍḍiyāna is by far the most frequently

[1] See *Nepal Catalogue*, Vol. II, p. 148, under 'Ṣoḍaśanityātantra':

तन्त्रं मदुक्तं भुवने नवनाथैरकल्पयत् ।
त्वया तैर्भुवने तन्त्रं कल्पे कल्पे विजृम्भते ॥

Also op. cit., Vol. I, preface, pp. lxxviii ff. That the Tantra came from outside India is suggested by the verse:

गच्छ त्वं भारते वर्षे अधिकाराय सर्वतः । पीठोपपीठक्षेत्रेषु कुरु सृष्टिमनेकधा ॥

[2] pp. 453, 455.

[3] Mr. H. E. Stapleton, Director of Public Instruction, Bengal, who was very intimately connected with Assam, suggested to me that Pūrṇagiri may very conveniently be identified with the ancient site of Puṇyatīrtha, in Assam.

mentioned among the four Pīṭhas, and its exact situation has been a matter of great controversy. Waddell[1] identified Uḍḍiyāna with Udyāna in the Swat valley. The Tibetan scholar, S. C. Das, followed in his footsteps.[2] M. Sylvain Levi would place Uḍḍiyāna somewhere in Kashgarh. Mm. Haraprasād Śāstrī definitely identifies Uḍḍiyāna with Orissa. In view of this wide divergence of opinion amongst scholars of high reputation, it is necessary to enter into the question in detail and examine it carefully. Indrabhūti is described as a king of Uḍḍiyāna, and Guru Padmasambhava, who went to Tibet to help Śāntarakṣita in founding the great monastery at Samye, is described as the son of Indrabhūti.[3] Padmasambhava married a sister of Śāntarakṣita in the latter's native place at Zāhor,[4] when driven away by his father (Indrabhūti) for killing some of his favourite subjects. This Zāhor is identified with the modern village of Sābhār, in the district of Dacca in Eastern Bengal.[5] Śāntarakṣita belonged to the royal family of Zāhor, and, therefore, it is hardly possible that the king of this place would allow his daughter to be married to an unknown vagabond, who came from such a distant place as Kashgarh, or Udyāna in Swat, being driven out of the kingdom. This marriage can be explained only if Uḍḍiyāna and Zāhor are taken to be nearer to each other. Moreover, Uḍḍiyāna is mentioned along with Kāmākhyā and Sirihaṭṭa, which, as we can see, are very near each other; and it is hardly possible that Uḍḍiyāna would be associated in Buddhist books with the other two if the distance were very considerable.[6]

[1] *Lamaism*, p. 380.

[2] S. C. Das wrongly writes Udyāna for Uḍḍiyāna, as he might have thought the two to be definitely identical.

[3] *Lamaism*, p. 380.

[4] op. cit., p. 382. Zā-hor is identified by Waddell as Lahore, with a query after it.

[5] I am indebted to Mr. N. K. Bhaṭṭaśālī for this identification.

[6] cf. Waddell, op. cit., p. 382: 'and to the cemetery of Laṅkā (crtsegs-pa),

Uḍḍiyāna, according to the authority of the *Pag Sam Jon Zan*,[1] is the place where Tāntric Buddhism first developed. In the history of the 84 Siddhas,[2] Uḍḍiyāna is described as a country containing 500,000 towns, and divided into two kingdoms. In one, called Sambhala, Indrabhūti ruled; while the other, Laṅkāpuri,[3] was in the occupation of Jalendra, whose son had for his wife Indrabhūti's sister, Lakṣmīṅkarā. When she became a Siddha, after being initiated by Indrabhūti, the latter retired after handing over the kingdom to his son.

This also does not clear up our difficulties; but the identification of Uḍḍiyāna becomes dependent on that of Laṅkāpuri, which is generally identified with either a peak in the Amarakaṇṭaka mountain, or a place in Assam or Central India or Ceylon.[4] But Laṅkā has never been even remotely considered in the northernmost or the westernmost part of India, such as either Kashgarh or Swat. Now, if we accept the identification of Laṅkā in Assam, then Uḍḍiyāna will have to be located in the same country, probably in the western part of it; and this seems to be more likely, as Kāmākhyā and Sylhet are both situated in Assam, which until recently formed part of the province of Bengal.

Moreover, Luipā, who is regarded as one of the earliest Siddhācāryas, is described in the *Pag Sam Jon Zan*[5] as a member of the fisherman caste who rose to be the writer in the employ of the king of Uḍḍiyāna and was then known as Samantaśubha. He met Śabarīpā, who initiated him into the mysteries of Tāntrism.

in the Zā-hor, where he was named "Padmasambhava". Note this Laṅkā was a part of the kingdom of Uḍḍiyāna.

[1] op. cit., index, p. cxli.

[2] *Tārānātha*, p. 325.

[3] Note in Waddell, op. cit., p. 382, Laṅkā is associated with Zā-hor.

[4] I.H.Q., Vol. II, June, p. 354.

[5] op. cit., index, p. cxv.

In the Tangyur catalogue[1] Luipā is characterized as a Mahāyogīśvara, and, what is important, as a Bengali.

Luipā composed a number of songs in the Bengali language, which have been discovered and published in the *Bauddha Gān O Dohā*,[2] with a short account of the author and his songs in the introduction. Luipā seems to have composed a book of songs, entitled the *Luhipādagītikā*, which is now preserved in Tibetan translation only, and from which only a few songs are extant in the original language.

There is then an apparent discrepancy in the two statements of the native place of Luipā. The testimony of the *Pag Sam Jon Zan* would take it to Uḍḍiyāna; while the Tangyur catalogue will have it in Bengal. There is, however, no real discrepancy in the two statements, because Luipā can both belong to Uḍḍiyāna and still be a Bengali. On the circumstances enumerated above, and the identification of Uḍḍiyāna not being settled, it is quite possible to locate it in Bengal. If, however, Laṅkāpuri—the counterpart of Uḍḍiyāna—is located, according to Prof. Jacobi, in Assam, then Uḍḍiyāna also will have to be located in Assam, possibly in the western part of it, which is also a part of Bengal.[3]

It is, then, in Uḍḍiyāna that Tāntrism first developed, and was probably transmitted to the other Pīṭhas, Kāmākhyā, Sirihaṭṭa and Pūrṇagiri (which must be somewhere near), and thence to the rest of India.

[1] P. Cordier, *Catalogue du Fonds Tibétain de la Bibliothèque Nationale*, 2 partie, p. 33, under No. xii, 8.

[2] Published by the Vaṅgīya Sāhitya Pariṣad, Calcutta, under the editorship of Mm. Haraprasād Śāstrī. See intro., p. 20.

[3] In the *Sādhanamālā*, pp. 80 and 83, Sarahapā is also associated with Uḍḍiyāna. This Sarahapā was one of the earliest Siddhācāryas. In the *Bauddha Gān O Dohā* are recorded a number of his songs, composed in the Bengali language. He is said to have been born in the Kingdom of Rājñī (?), in Eastern India.

CHAPTER VI

THE TANTRAS

BOTH Hindus and Buddhists were alike prolific writers of the Tantras, and the extant literature on them is wonderfully extensive. One of the reasons why the word Tantra cannot be defined, but can only be described, is because of the fact that an astonishing number of subjects comes within its purview, not to speak of its own numerous subdivisions. The Buddhist Tantras in outward appearance resemble the Hindu Tantras to a marked degree, but in reality there is very little similarity between them, either in the subject matter or in the philosophical doctrines inculcated in them, or in religious principles. This is not to be wondered at, since the aims and objects of the Buddhists are widely different from those of the Hindus. It is difficult to determine when and under what circumstances the word Tantra came to be employed in the sense in which it is used in this literature; nor is it possible to trace the origin of the Tantras or of the people who first introduced them. To any careful student of Tāntric literature it will be evident that when magical practices become extremely popular with one section of Indian population the other sections take them up and incorporate them into their religion, mostly in a modified form to suit their own requirements and tenets; and this process of emergence and relapsing goes on continually. The Vedic sacrifices, as performed by the orthodox Brāhmaṇic society in the very earliest times, attracted a large number of converts from among the Vrātyas; and it can be very easily imagined, from the practice obtaining in the present time, that people in those days looked upon the sacrifices, and the Brāhmaṇas performing them, with superstitious awe and reverence. The sacrifices were at one time very popular, specially in the pre-Buddhistic period; and, as a matter of fact, no undertaking of any consequence was hazarded without a sacrifice immediately preceding it. Sacrifices were performed mostly for obtaining happiness in this, the next, and future lives. The results of these sacrifices could, under the circumstances, never be ascertained with scientific regularity, and it appears, therefore, all the more strange that sacrifices, even in modern times, should be so popular in Southern India, especially in Travancore, and that we should hear even now of sacrifices being performed on a gigantic scale and at an enormous cost. Buddhism came in when sacrifices were the order of the day; when numerous animals were immolated and eaten in monstrous assemblies. In Aśoka's time also we find sacrifices and the free use of meat in the assemblies very popular. That the very first of a long series of rock-edicts of Aśoka should deal with the stoppage of such assemblies displays the great influence sacrifices, with their cooked meat, exercised on the minds of the Indian population, including the Brāhmaṇas. It is no wonder, therefore, that, on the dismemberment of the Mauryan empire, the sacrifices prohibited by the great Buddhist emperor should be revived with great vigour under the Sāmavedī Śuṅgas, who performed two sacrifices[1] on a grand scale in the very capital of the king who had insulted the orthodox sacrifice. Though Buddha was antagonistic to all sorts of sacrifices, necromancy, sorcery or magic, he is credited, nevertheless, with having given instructions concerning Mudrās, Maṇḍalas and Tantras, etc., so that by virtue of these prosperity in this world could be attained by his less advanced disciples, who seemed to care more for this world than for the Nirvāṇa preached by him. India in Buddha's time was so steeped in superstitions that any religion which dared forbid all kinds of magic, sorcery and necromancy could hardly hope to withstand popular opposition. A clever organizer, as

[1] J.B.O.R.S., K. P. Jayaswal, 'An Inscription of the Śuṅga Dynasty', Vol. X, p. 205.

Buddha was, he did not fail to notice the importance of incorporating magical practices in his religion to make it popular from all points of view and attract more adherents thereby. Up till now we were ignorant of Buddha's attitude towards the Tāntric practices, excepting a few meagre references in Pāli literature, and were unable to determine the time of their introduction in Buddhism. But Śāntarakṣita (A.D. 705–762) and his disciple Kamalaśīla brought out this connexion very forcibly in the *Tattvasaṁgraha*[1] and its commentary, stating fully the reasons which made Buddha incorporate them in his system. The Tantras and the mantras have been practised by the Buddhists since the time of Buddha; but, unfortunately, we do not possess any connected account of them. We only know that a few works on the Dhāraṇīs must have been in existence early in the beginning of the Christian era. The Dhāraṇīs are only unmeaning strings of words, which are said to confer great merit when muttered repeatedly. Then comes the worship of Buddha in the *Prajñāpāramitā*, with all the paraphernalia of worship, such as is to be found in the Tāntric worship, for obtaining worldly happiness. Then follows the different recensions of the *Prajñāpāramitā*: the Sūtra, the Hṛdayasūtra with its Dhāraṇīs and mantras, recitations of all of which are able to confer the benefit of reading the whole of the *Prajñāpāramitā*. Contemporaneous with the *Prajñāpāramitā* is the *Mañjuśrīmūlakalpa*, where Mañjuśrī in a princely form is worshipped in a Maṇḍala, with all the paraphernalia of worship and an immense number of Mudrās, mantras and Dhāraṇīs. Later on, in the *Guhyasamāja*, the five Dhyāni Buddhas, with a Śakti attached to each, are found described in a Maṇḍala, and a number of secret and immoral practices introduced.

On the side of Hinduism, the Paurāṇic literature attracted a

[1] op. cit., p. 905. तदुक्तमन्त्रयोगादि ० ।

large number of people, by its wonderful stories holding out a promise of an award of merits to be gained by hearing it, and practising the rites and observances recommended therein, and worshipping the gods described in it. The Purāṇas in a very popular form continued to wield vigorously their influence on the minds of only the superstitious people of India, right up to the time of the Muhammadan conquest; and after that, in a more or less acute form, up to the present time. The flood of mighty western civilization may generally be held responsible for the total annihilation of public discourses on the Purāṇas and allied literature in many parts of Eastern India; the same forces are now at work everywhere in other parts of India also.

Moreover, the conception of gods and goddesses in the Paurāṇic literature was so very attractive that the Buddhists in later times could not help incorporating the idea of godhead into their religion; and when they actually did this they deified all important personalities of Buddhism, together with the deification of a large number of abstract ideas and philosophical concepts, and included a few purely Hindu gods such as Gaṇeśa, Sarasvatī, etc., in their pantheon. The Buddhists busied themselves with producing a variety of literature on the Tantras, and during the Tāntric age thousands of works were written. These works were readily transmitted through the Himalayan passes to Tibet and Mongolia, and thence to China and Japan, and their influence made a large section of population in these countries believers in gross magic and abject superstition. It is not strange, therefore, that many of these Tāntric works, whose originals in Sanskrit are lost, are now preserved in translations in the pages of the Tibetan Tangyur. The developments in Tantra made by the Buddhists, and the extraordinary plastic art they developed, did not fail to create an impression also on the minds of the Hindus, who readily incorporated many ideas, doctrines, practices and gods, originally conceived by the Buddhists for their religion. The literature, which goes by the name of the Hindu Tantras, arose almost immediately after the Buddhist ideas had established themselves; though after the Tāntric age, even up to the last century, Tāntric works continued to be written by Hindus.

Having thus given a survey of the history of Tāntric literature and the mutual interchange of ideas, doctrines and concepts, we will now proceed to give a definition, or rather a description, of what is ordinarily meant by the word Tantra. Many scholars have tried to define and describe the Tantras; but each and every one of their descriptions is incomplete and insufficient. They are bound to be so, because the writers of the Tantras were most erratic and never followed any definite plan. Moreover, the definition which holds good in the case of the Hindu Tantras is not found adequate when applied to the Buddhist branch of this literature. Therefore, the definitions of Tantra, as given by critical students of Sanskrit literature, are not unlike the description of an elephant given by a number of blind men.

The Hindus will not call any work a Tantra[1] which does not include the following subjects among many others: stories of the creation and the destruction of the world, mystic charms, description of the abode of gods and of holy places, the duties of men in the four stages of life and the position of the Brāhmaṇas, description of the abode of ghosts and other nocturnal beings, the mystic figures, the origin of magicians, the celestial trees, position of the stars, discourses on old stories, meanings of technical terms, vows and observations, differentiations of purity and impurity, enumeration of the characteristics of males and females, an account of the duties of kings, the customs of the age, and the rules of law, besides other spiritual subjects. The Hindus distinguish this śāstra from two others of a similar nature, which are known by the names of Āgama and Yāmala. They treat

[1] See *Sādhanamālā*, Vol. II (G.O.S., No. XLVI), intro., p. xix f.

of certain subjects which are not covered by the description of the Tantra given above. The Āgama,[1] to be called an Āgama, must include, besides the stories of the creation and the destruction of the world, the mode of worshipping gods and goddesses and the way of obtaining perfection and repetition of mantra according to a definite number, the practise of six cruel rites, and four kinds of meditation and austerity. The literature, which is known as Yāmala,[2] contains an account of creation, astronomical speculations, daily ceremonies, the order of festivals, technical aphorisms, division of four castes and various subcastes, and the customs and manners of the time.

The characteristics of Tantra, Yāmala and Āgama are given in almost every important Hindu Tāntric work. The definitions are not all alike and rarely give a complete idea; and all the definitions, taken together, will not suffice to give a true account of the entire contents of this enormous literature. In the definitions given above it will be seen that speculations on alchemy, medicine, divination, astrology, horoscopy, and many similar pseudo-scientific subjects, which frequently make their appearance in the Tāntric literature, are not included in the definitions of the word Tantra.

Similar features present themselves in the Tantras of the Buddhists, and the range of the numerous subjects treated of in this literature will be evidenced by the *Catalogue of the Tibetan Tangyur*, in the Bibliothèque Nationale, in Paris, compiled by P. Cordier. To understand the bulk of the Tāntric literature of the Buddhists, we must first take into account the fact that it is distributed among the three great divisions into which the later Buddhism was divided—namely, the Vajrayāna, Sahajayāna and Kālacakrayāna. Besides these there are other minor Yānas with no marked individuality, such as the Tantra

[1] ibid., p. xx. [2] ibid., p. xxi.

Yāna, the Mantra Yāna, the Bhadra Yāna, etc., which may be said to have originated from the Vajrayāna—the principal Yāna among the three mentioned above. Moreover, we must also consider the numerous sub-divisions of each of these three powerful Yānas and many less powerful systems, in all of which the Buddhist Tāntric literature was deeply interested. The Tāntric literature was mainly written by the Vajrayānists, who called themselves Vajrācāryas; and by the Siddhas, whose number is reputed to be eighty-four.

Without associating ourselves with the views expressed by an eminent authority on later Buddhism, let us close this chapter with the definition and the origin of Tantra given by Mahāmahopādhyāya Harapasād Śāstrī as early as 1911, in his introduction to N. N. Vasu's *Modern Buddhism and Its Followers in Orissa.* There he writes: 'The word Tantra is very loosely used. Ordinary people understand by it any system other than the Vedas. But it really means the worship of Śakti, or female energy. The female energy is worshipped in conjunction with male energy. The union of male and female is the essence of Tantra.'[1]

This definition truly applies to the advanced Buddhist Tantras of the Yogatantra and Anuttarayogatantra classes described in sequel, but it cannot be said to apply to the lower forms of Tantra, such as the Kriyātantrayāna or the Caryātantrayāna, nor is the definition all-embracing so as to include all classes of Tāntric literature, such as the Sādhana, Dhāraṇī, Stava, Homa, Maṇḍala, etc.

But what the same veteran scholar has said regarding the origin of Tantra is well worth considering by all students of Tantra, Hindu or Buddhist. He has said: 'Tantra came from outside India. Most probably it came with Magi priests of the Scythians. In the old Saṁhitās such as the *Niḥśvāsa-tattva*

[1] op. cit., p. 10.

Saṁhitā wonder is expressed at the novel mode of initiation enjoined by the Tantras. Vedic initiation was known, but people wondered how there could be a new initiation other than Vedic. It came from outside India and spread on the outskirts of the Aryan world. The five original places of Tantra in India are Jālandhara, Punā (Pūrṇagiri), Śrīparvata, Oḍiyāna and Kāmākhyā.'[1] The Magi origin of Tantra is a brilliant suggestion, though materials are not now sufficient to prove this contention. Asaṅga—the originator of Tantra in Buddhism—is reputed to be a Gāndhārian, and it is no wonder that he drew the inspiration from the Magi priests of Scythian origin. The Magi priests must have introduced the Śakti worship, or the union of male and female energies, and in the time of Asaṅga the ground was well prepared to receive this introduction, which was not known before the time of Asaṅga and that of the *Guhyasamāja*, either in the Dhāraṇī treatises or even the *Ārya-Mañjuśrīmūlakalpa*. This introduction for the first time found expression in the *Guhyasamājatantra*, where the theory of the five Dhyāni Buddhas was for the first time systematized, and each was assigned a Śakti for the purposes of union.

[1] op. cit., pp. 10, 11.

CHAPTER VII

MANTRAS

THE mantras, or mystic syllables, constitute the backbone of Tāntric Esoterism and of Vajrayāna. They are of innumerable varieties, such as Bīja Hṛdaya, Upahṛdaya, Pūjā, Arghya, Puṣpa, Dīpa, Dhūpa, Naivedya, Netra, Śikhā, Astra, Rakṣā, and so forth. These mantras are mostly a string of unmeaning words, but they sometimes disclose distinctly the influence of a language now unknown.[1] It is, however, impossible to say how these mantras were introduced into ancient India. Vedic hymns were indeed called mantras; but they had their meaning. The Vajrayānists, of course, in several instances attempted to trace the origin of certain mantras which point unmistakably to Buddha himself as their originator.[2] The mantras of Vajrayāna seem to be a development of Dhāraṇīs contained in works such as the *Vidhyādharapiṭaka*, to which a reference has been given by Hiuen-thsang. The Dhāraṇīs, according to Kern,[3] existed in Buddhism from very ancient times, and seemed to have been introduced into Buddhism for the benefit of the less-advanced followers, who did not care so much for Nirvāṇa as they did for their material prosperity in this world. Such recruits to Buddhism were enjoined to read some of the Sūtras, which, however, proved to be beyond their intelligence. For their benefit these had to be shortened into Dhāraṇīs, and the lay-disciples were enjoined to commit them to memory. This

[1] See, for instance, the mantra of Jāṅgulī for the prevention and cure of snake-bites. *Sādhanamālā*, pp. 249–50.

[2] cf. *Sādhanamālā*, p. 334 : प्रज्ञादिसाधनमिदं सुगतोपदिष्टम् ।

p. 335 : स्वाहान्तः कथितः स एष सुगतैर्मन्त्रः कवित्वादिभूः ।

[3] *Manual of Buddhism*, p. 6.

seems to be the process in which Sūtras underwent a change in very ancient times, and, ultimately, when they were further reduced, they gave rise to mantra. To illustrate, let us take *Aṣṭasāhasrikāprajñāpāramitā*, which is in itself too stupendous for a tolerably learned Buddhist to read through and understand, not to speak of the illiterate masses, who were mostly responsible for the great popularity of the Mahāyāna. They could not, indeed, read this vast literature for acquiring merit; for them something shorter was necessary. *Prajñāpāramitā*, with its 8,000 stanzas, was therefore reduced to a hundred, and, ultimately, to a very few stanzas, which became known as the *Prajñāpāramitāhṛdayasūtra*, which was further reduced to make room for the *Prajñāpāramitādhāraṇī*. The next step in this chain of evolution was in the formation of a Prajñāpāramitā mantra, which again led to the conception of a Bīja in one syllable Praṁ, in response to which Śūnya may transform itself into the form of the goddess by name Prajñāpāramitā, who is a veritable metamorphosis of the Prajñāpāramitā literature. The evolution of the Tāntric mantra can be traced thus through its successive stages in the Buddhist literature. When, however, we turn our attention to Hindu literature, we are surprised to find that the Tāntric mantras suddenly make their entry into it without showing even a faint trace of the earlier and cruder stages of development. This seems to be a sufficient reason for believing the Hindu māntric system to be later than Vajrayāna, and for holding that the mantras were incorporated into Hinduism bodily from Buddhism.

Once again it becomes necessary to discuss the origin of the Buddhist mantras and point to their originator. It may be remembered that all the original Tāntric works of Buddhism are in the form of Saṅgītis, where Buddha is introduced in an assembly of the faithful; and where he delivers these Tantras, including the mantras and secret practices, and gives his reasons for not doing so earlier. The usual reason is, that he refrained from communicating the substance of the new Tantra earlier because people were not well-prepared to receive it.[1] This fact points unmistakably to Buddha as the originator of the Tantras, mantras, doctrines and the esoteric tenets and practices. In the *Sādhanamālā*, which is a collection of 312 short works called Sādhanas, and of which the earliest MS. bears a date in the Newari era which is equivalent to A.D. 1165, we find Sugata, or Buddha, mentioned as the originator of several powerful mantras. The Sādhana of Jāṅgulī, for instance, which is in the form of a Saṅgīti, is said to have been delivered by Buddha himself.[2] The Sādhana of Vajrasarasvatī is said to have been composed in accordance with the instructions of the Sugata. The Prajñāpāramitā mantra is said to have been delivered by Buddha himself. As already mentioned, the famous logician, Śāntarakṣita, and his erudite disciple, Kamalaśīla, both of whom belonged to the eighth century of the Christian era, are of opinion[3] that Buddha himself instructed the people in Mudrās, mantras, Maṇḍalas, etc., so that they might obtain prosperity in this world. From these evidences it is easy to conclude that Buddha introduced some sort of esoterism into his religion, which in later times, owing to a variety of influences, developed into a full-fledged esoteric system in the form of Vajrayāna.

The Vajrayānists maintain that the mantras are endowed with great powers and they blindly believe in them. In the Buddhist Tāntric literature passages showing this blind faith on their part are very frequent and eloquent. In one place it is said: 'What is there impossible for the mantras to perform, if they are applied according to rules?'[4] In another place it is said that,

[1] *Guhyasamāja*, G.O.S., chap. XVII, p. 144.

[2] *Sādhanamālā*, pp. 248 f., 334, 335.

[3] *Tattvasaṁgraha*, p. 905. Kamalaśīla says:
योगः समाधिः । आदिशब्देन मुद्रामण्डलादिपरिग्रहः ।

[4] *Sādhanamālā*, p. 575: किमस्त्यसाध्यं मन्त्राणां योजितानां यथाविधि ।

'through the repeated mutterings of the mantra, so much power is generated that it can astonish the whole world'.[1] The mantras by their power can even confer Buddha-hood. The merits that accrue from the mutterings of the mantra of Mahākāla are so numerous that all the Buddhas taken together cannot count them, even if they were to count without cessation for a number of days and nights. The five greatest sins, according to Buddhism, are the five Ānantaryas; but these can be easily washed away, and perfection can be gained, if the mantra of Lokanātha is repeated. By the repetition of the mantra of Khasarpaṇa Buddha-hood becomes as easy of access as the Badaraka fruit in the palm of the hand. By the Dhāraṇī of Avalokiteśvara even an ass can keep at least 300 stanzas in memory. The mantra of Ekajaṭā[2] is said to be so powerful that the moment it is muttered the person becomes free from danger, is always followed by good fortune, his enemies are all destroyed, and without doubt he becomes as pious as Buddha. Examples such as these can easily be multiplied. Lest the people prove doubting, which they are always apt to be with regard to such mystic matters, the Tantras from time to time give the assurance that the power of the mind is extraordinary, and one should not doubt, therefore, what has been said about the efficacy of the mantras.[3]

It is said the mantras are only powerful when they are applied strictly in accordance with the rules. In fact, the rules are so strict and minute and so numerous that it is quite impossible that any mantra is capable of being applied by ordinary mortals in strict conformity to them; and this is a factor which is apt to discourage the enthusiasm of the new recruits. 'You should not be sorry,' says Kumudākaramati, 'because you are not able to

[1] ibid., p. 334. विश्वविस्मापने शक्तिरस्मादस्योपजायते ।

[2] ibid., p. 262. देव्या एकजटायास्तु मन्त्रराजो महाबलः ।, etc.

[3] ibid., p. 330. संशयो नहि कर्तव्यो विचित्रा भावशक्तयः ।

apply the mantra in accordance with the rules stated before. At least you should perform the rite of self-protection and think of the closure of the boundary and of worship, and repeat the mantra as long as you can and aim at perfection. In accordance with your powers and actions you will certainly obtain results. The testimony of the Tantras, in this connection, is that such a worshipper can alone give protection to the world.'[1] The repetition of the mantras has to be done with the greatest care, and the Tantras give direction for their proper repetition. For instance, they should not be repeated too quickly or too slowly. The mind at the time of repetition should be free from all impure reflections and should be completely concentrated on the letters of the mantra, which should be repeated so long as there is no tired feeling.[2]

The mantras are considered most sacred by the Vajrayānists; and their accuracy was jealously guarded by them, in much the same way as the purity of the Vedic mantras was maintained by means of several ingenious devices. These mantras are composed usually in ordinary prose, but occasionally in an enigmatic language, the meaning of which sometimes becomes very difficult to understand. The mantras are done into prose and mnemonic verses for the obvious purpose of memorizing. These verses are extremely curious and give practically no meaning to ordinary readers. Let us take, for instance, the verse—

आदौ चक्रधरस्ततः पिचुयुगात् प्रज्ञान्वितो वर्धनि
तस्माच्च ज्वलयुग्ममस्य च परे मेधा परे वर्धनि ।
एतस्माच्चरमं धिरिव्दयमतो बुध्दिस्तथा वर्धनि
स्वाहान्तः कथितः स एष सुगतैर्मन्त्रः कवित्वादिभूः ॥

[1] ibid., p. 13. यथोक्तेनाहं शक्त इति नावसादितव्यं ।, etc.

[2] ibid., p. 10. न द्रुतं न बिलम्बितं असत्सङ्कल्पवर्जितं मन्त्राक्षरगतचित्तं तावज्जपेत् यावत् खेदो न भवति ।

When translated, it will have the following meaning:[1]

> In the beginning there is the holder of the disc, who is followed by two Picus and Vardhani joined with Prajñā. After that there are two Jvalas, which are followed by Vardhani after Medhā; even at the end there are two Dhiris, Buddhi and Vardhani ending in Svāhā. This mantra, which has the power to confer the cleverness of a poet, was introduced by the Sugata.

At first sight the verse gives no meaning, unless you know that it is the statement of a mantra which refers to Vajravīṇāsarasvatī and runs as:

ॐ पिचु पिचु प्रज्ञावर्धनि ज्वल ज्वल मेधावर्धनि धिरि धिरि बुध्दिवर्धनि स्वाहा ।

There were other ways of preserving the accuracy of mantras, by dissecting the letters and expressing each of them by means of symbols. Two examples of this kind are given below.

First, let us take the mantra of Sarasvatī, which is expressed in the following mnemonic verse:

सप्तमस्य व्दितीयस्थमष्टमस्य चतुर्थकम् ।
प्रथमस्य चतुर्थेन भूषितं तत् सबिन्दुकम् ॥ [2]

> It stands on the second of the seventh and is the fourth of the eighth; it is accompanied by the fourth of the first and is decorated with the spot.

The explanation seems to be: the second syllable of the seventh class (Antaḥstha) is Ra; fourth of the eighth (Uṣma) is Ha; fourth of the first (Svara) is Ī; the spot is ∸ Anusvara; therefore the resultant Bīja is HRĪṀ, which is the Bīja of Sarasvatī.

Let us take the mantra of Ekajaṭā, as expressed in a mnemonic verse, as the second example:

[1] ibid., p. 335. [2] ibid., p. 335.

हान्तं हुताशनस्थं च चतुर्थस्वरभेदितम् ।
बिन्दुमस्तकसंभिन्नं खण्डेन्दुसहितं पुनः ॥
एतद्बीजं महब्दीजं व्दितीयं शृणु साम्प्रतम् ।
तान्तं वन्हिसमायुक्तं पुनस्तेनैव भेदितम् ॥
नादबिन्दुसमायुक्तं व्दितीयं भवति स्थिरम् ।
तृतीयं तु पुनर्बीजं कथयामि प्रयत्नतः ॥
हान्तं षष्टस्वराक्रान्तं नादबिन्दुसमन्वितम् ।
एतद्बीजवरं श्रेष्ठ त्रैलोक्यदहनात्मकम् ॥
कथयामि चतुर्थं च यथा बुध्देन भाषितम् ।
फान्तं शुध्दं सुतेजाढ्यं सर्व्वसिध्दिप्रदायकम् ॥
शृणु अर्धाक्षरं सम्यक् मन्तनिष्पत्तिकारणम् ।
टान्तमविहीनं तु उच्चारेण तु रक्षणम् ॥ [1]

It ends in H, placed on fire, is pierced by the fourth vowel, and is accompanied by spots and the half-moon. This Bīja is a great Bīja. Now hear of the second, which ends in T with fire, is pierced by the same and is accompanied by Nādabindu. The third also I state carefully, which ends in H trampling on the sixth vowel and is accompanied by Nādabindu. This Bīja is the most powerful and is able to set the three worlds on fire. I state now, as was done before by Buddha, the fourth syllable which ends in Pha and gives all kinds of perfections. In order to complete the mantra hear the half syllable ending in Ṭa, which is deprived of its A and by mere utterance saves all.

First Bīja consists of H R (fire) Ī (fourth vowel) Ḥ (spots) Ṁ, and the resultant syllable is Hrīṁh(s). The second Bīja includes T R (fire) Ī and Ṁ, which together makes Trīṁ. The third has H Ū (sixth vowel) and Ṁ, which together give Hūṁ. The fourth is Pha, while the fifth letter is Ṭa, which is deprived of its A and therefore considered as a half letter. The last two will give Phaṭ. So the whole mantra stands as: Hrīṁ Strīṁ Hūṁ Phaṭ.

[1] ibid., p. 261 f.

CHAPTER VIII

SOME PROMINENT AUTHORS

NEVER before has an attempt been made to construct a chronology of Tāntric authors: probably because the Vajrayāna is a field of literature entirely unexplored. It is hazardous, indeed, to make an attempt of that kind, and any research made in the beginning is likely to be faulty and not altogether free from error. Even so, it is necessary to make an attempt in order that the development of Tāntric ideas, doctrines and practices may be more fully appreciated.

Very little is known regarding the Tantras before they made a début in a well-developed form in the beginning of the Tāntric period, which began in about the middle of the seventh century A.D. It is bound to be so, because the Tantras, as has already been pointed out, were practised in secret and handed down in secret through an unbroken chain of preceptors and disciples,[1] who never made themselves known, and, as such, passed out of recognition.

All that we know of the earlier period is that the *Mañjuśrī-mūlakalpa*, which was earlier than the *Guhyasamāja*, was probably written in the second century A.D., or even earlier; that the *Guhyasamāja* was written in the time of Asaṅga, in the third century A.D., and that Asaṅga composed a sādhana of Prajñā-pāramitā,[2] where he made a definite reference to the five Dhyāni Buddhas and their consorts In the later period, however, there are more materials for constructing the chronology of Vajrayāna. These consist, mainly, of a few important succession lists of gurus and disciples, and some fragmentary accounts

[1] *Tārānātha*, 201. [2] *Sādhanamālā*, p. 321.

found in the work of Tārānātha and the *Pag Sam Jon Zan.* One of the successions is as follows:

1. Padmavajra.	5. Līlāvajra.
2. Anaṅgavajra.	6. Dārikapā.
3. Indrabhūti.	7. Sahajayoginī Cintā.
4. Bhagavatī Lakṣmī.	8. Ḍombī Heruka.[1]

The second succession list, on which we can rely for the present, is the list given by Kazi Dawasamdup, in his Introduction to the *Cakrasamvara Tantra.* The succession given here is stated as follows:

1. Saraha.	5. Vajraghaṇṭā.	9. Guhya.
2. Nāgārjuna.	6. Kacchapā.	10. Vijayapā.
3. Śabaripā.	7. Jālandharipā.	. . . . .
4. Luipā.	8. Kṛṣṇācārya.	11. Tailopā.
		12. Nāropā.[2]

It is natural to assume that the Tāntric gurus were particular about their succession lists, and each important Tantra may be believed to have a succession list of this kind. When these Tantras were translated into Tibetan, the translators occasionally noted the tradition of the Tantras, as it was handed down through a succession of gurus and disciples. It is in this way that some lists have been preserved and at present constitute our chief authentic material in determining the chronology of this extensive literature.

Further landmarks are furnished by an important statement made by Tārānātha, in his *History of Buddhism*, with regard to the introduction of some original Tantras by one or other of the Siddhācāryas. While mentioning the origin of some of the most important Tantras, Tārānātha gives us the information that Saraha

[1] *Catalogue du Fonds Tibétain de la Bibliothèque Nationale par P. Cordier*, 2e partie, p. 211 f.

[2] Arthur Avalon's Tāntric Texts: *Śhrīcakrasambhāratantra*, edited by Kazi Dawasamdup, intro., p. xxxv. °sambhāra stands for Sanskrit °samvara.

introduced the *Būddhakapālatantra*, Luipā the *Yoginīsañcaryā*, Kambala and Padmavajra the *Hevajratantra*, Kṛṣṇācārya the *Samputatilaka*, Lalitavajra the *Kṛṣṇayamāritantra*, Gambhīravajra the *Vajrāmṛtatantra*, Kukkurīpā the *Mahāmāyātantra*, and Piṭo (?) the *Kālacakratantra*.[1]

With these materials in hand, let us attempt to determine the chronology by assigning a definite time to some of the more familiar authors, and fix the time of others by assuming an interval of twelve years backwards or forwards. The two lists given above are pretty long, covering a considerable period, and seem to be fairly authentic, though not altogether correct. In these two lists there are several points of contact; one is represented by Jālandharipā, who was the first in the second list to profess the *Hevajratantra* and to compose a work on the subject. The *Hevajratantra* was introduced by Padmavajra of the first list, who must, therefore, be earlier than Jālandharipā by at least one generation. The second point of contact is that Kamalaśīla, who was removed by one generation from Indrabhūti, wrote a book in which he closely followed a commentary composed by Saraha.[2] The third point of contact is that Dārikapā in one of his songs reverentially mentions the name of Luipā, who must, therefore, be earlier.

Now in the first list the name of Indrabhūti, whose time has been almost definitely fixed, is well known. He was the father of Guru Padmasambhava, who, along with Śāntarakṣita, the author of the *Tattvasaṁgraha*, went to Tibet on an invitation from the contemporary king, and erected a monastery at Samye in the year A.D. 749, on the model of the Odantapuri Vihāra.[3] If we take Padmasambhava to be thirty years of age when he went to Tibet in the year A.D. 747, then Indrabhūti's time will be approximately

[1] *Tāranātha*, p. 275 f.

[2] *Catalogue du Fonds Tibétain*, 2e partie, p. 248.

[3] Waddell, *Lamaism*, p. 379 et seq.; see also *Tattvasaṁgraha*, Foreword, pp. x ff.

fixed to a period between A.D. 687 and A.D. 717 onwards. If we take A.D. 717 as the starting-point, and twelve years between each succession of a guru and his disciple, the approximate timing of the first succession list will be as follows:

1.	Padmavajra	A.D. 693
2.	Anaṅgavajra	„ 705
3.	Indrabhūti	„ 717
4.	Lakṣmīṅkarā	„ 729
5.	Līlāvajra	„ 741
6.	Dārikapā	„ 753
7.	Sahajayoginī	„ 765
8.	Ḍombī Heruka	„ 777

If Jālandharipā is taken to be removed by only one generation from Padmavajra, who introduced the *Hevajratantra* for the first time, and an interval of twelve years is taken between each succession, the chronological order of the second succession will be as follows:

1.	Saraha	A.D. 633
2.	Nāgārjuna	„ 645
3.	Śabaripā	„ 657
4.	Luipā	„ 669
5.	Vajraghaṇṭā	„ 681
6.	Kacchapā	„ 693
7.	Jālandharipā	„ 705
8.	Kṛṣṇācārya	„ 717
9.	Guhya	„ 729
10.	Vijayapā	„ 741

With regard to Tailopā and Nāropā, it may be assumed that the list does not furnish correct information, as we are able to check its veracity from other sources. Between Vijayapā and Tailopā, therefore, there must have been many intermediate gurus who are not mentioned.

It is well known that Tailopā was a contemporary of Mahīpāla, probably the first Mahīpāla of the Pāla dynasty of Bengal, who flourished between A.D. 978 and 1030; while Nāropā succeeded Jetāri, also a contemporary of Mahīpāla, as a Dvārapaṇḍita of Vikramaśīla.[1] Therefore *circa* A.D. 978 may be assigned to Tailopā and A.D. 990 to his disciple Nāropā.

When we fix the time of Saraha, we practically go to the root of the Buddhist Tantra or Tantrayāna, because Saraha is reputed to be one of the chief promulgators of the Tāntric religion. Both Tārānātha and the author of the *Pag Sam Jon Zan* admit that Saraha was one of the earliest writers and diffusers of Tāntric doctrines and practices. While mentioning the origin of the Tantras, Tārānātha places Saraha's *Buddhakapālatantra* as the first in his list. Saraha's name has also been placed on the top of the succession list of a Tantra of no less celebrity than the *Cakrasamvaratantra.* Saraha was one of the Siddhas to popularize the Tantra. The Tantra, which was practised in secret from the time of Asaṅga, or even from the time of Buddha, first got publicity through the teachings of a band of Siddhas, with Saraha at their head.

1. SARAHA (A.D. 633)

According to the author of the *Pag Sam Jon Zan,*[2] Saraha, or Rāhulabhadra, was the name of a Buddhist sage born of a Brāhmaṇ and a Ḍākinī in the city of Rajñī (?), in the Eastern country. He was an adept both in the Brāhmaṇical and the Buddhist lores, and flourished during the reign of Candanapāla of Prācya. He worked some miracles in the presence of King Ratnaphala and his Brāhmaṇ minister, and thereby converted them to the Buddhist faith. Afterwards he became the high priest of Nālandā. It is also related of him that he visited Orissa, where, from one Covesakalpa, he learnt the Mantrayāna, and from there proceeded to Mahārāṣṭra. There he united in Yoga with a female ascetic, who had approached him

[1] *Pag Sam Jon Zan*, index, pp. xli, lv. [2] index, p. xxvi.

in the guise of an archer's daughter. Having performed the Mahāmudrā ritual of mysticism, he attained perfection. He was thenceforward known as Siddha Saraha. He used to sing the Dohā hymns of mysticism, and thereby converted five thousand people and their king to Buddhism. Saraha composed a large number of verses in Sanskrit, and their translations are preserved in the pages of the Tibetan Tangyur. Saraha was also known as Sarahabhadra and Rāhulabhadra, and was one of the earliest Buddhists responsible for diffusing the Tāntric knowledge and popularizing it. It is noteworthy that the time assigned to him, according to the new calculation, makes him a contemporary of Dharmakīrti (A.D. 600–50) during or after whose time, according to Tārānātha, the Tantras got publicity.

2. NĀGĀRJUNA (A.D 645)

The next author in importance is Nāgārjuna, who is, of course, different from the author of the same name who is regarded as the founder of the Madhyamaka school of Buddhist philosophy. Absurd accounts are recorded about the life of this Nāgārjuna; and wild stories are told of his stupendous magical feats. M. Walleser,[1] after a thorough investigation of the accounts of Nāgārjuna from Tibetan and Chinese sources, has come to the conclusion that there was no such person as Nāgārjuna; and that he was a pure myth. From his learned and scholarly observations it can be easily seen that the Tibetan sources have hopelessly mixed up together the accounts of Nāgārjuna—the disciple of Aśvaghoṣa, with Nāgārjuna—the disciple of Saraha. One flourished in the first and the second quarter of the second century; while the other flourished in the middle of the seventh century, the two names thus being separated by five hundred years. But as these two persons are taken erroneously to be the same, a serious confusion has arisen. The Chinese version, which

[1] *The Life of Nāgārjuna, from Tibetan and Chinese Sources*, p. 1.

does not take into account the Tāntric Nāgārjuna, is less confusing, though it also abounds in absurd stories about his life. We are not, however, concerned here with the accounts of Nāgārjuna the founder of the Madhyamaka school; but it can be easily proved that the second or the Tāntric Nāgārjuna is a historical person and a follower of Vajrayāna. Two Sādhanas of his are recorded in the *Sādhanamālā*, one for the worship of Vajratāra, while the other relates to the worship of Ekajaṭā.[1] In the colophon of the latter, it is distinctly said that Nāgārjuna rescued this Sādhana from the country of Bhoṭa, which is identified with Tibet.[2] Nāgārjuna was a leading star in the Vajrayāna horizon, and composed a large number of Tāntric works, the translations of many of which have been preserved in the Tibetan Tangyur.[3]

3. ŚABARIPĀ OR ŚABARAPĀ (A.D. 657)

Śabaripā is the third author in chronological order. He is described in Tibetan works[4] as belonging to the hill-tribe called the Śabaras, or the huntsmen, in Bāṅgālā, where he met Nāgārjuna during the latter's residence in that country, and embraced Tāntrism, and, after being initiated by him along with his two wives, Lokī and Guṇī, attained sainthood. This Śabaripā also must have been a historical person, as he has composed a Sādhana of Kurukullā, which was published in the *Sādhanamālā* for the first time.[5] This Sādhana is found in only one manuscript, namely, the one from Cambridge University, which bears a date in the Newari era equivalent to A.D. 1165. He is also the author of a number of melodious songs in the vernacular of his country, which, according to the Tibetan authorities, was Bāṅgālā, or Bengal.

[1] op. cit., pp. 193 f. and 265 f.

[2] आर्यनागार्जुनपादैर्भोटेषु उध्दृतम् ।

[3] See infra, chap. VIII.

[4] For instance, in *Pag Sam Jon Zan*, index, p. cxxxi.

[5] op. cit., p. 385.

4. LUIPĀ (A.D. 669)

Luipā is our next author in chronological order. He is termed the first Siddhācārya, or magician; and is even now respected as such, and in the Tangyur Catalogue he is distinctly called a Bengali.[1] In other Tibetan books he is further said to have sprung from the fisherman caste of Uḍḍiyāna, and was very fond of the entrails of fish. He was formerly a clerk in the employ of the king of Uḍḍiyāna; and was known as Samantaśubha.[2] He composed many mystic songs, and several Dohās of his are recorded in the *Bauddha Gān O Dohā*.

5. PADMAVAJRA (A.D. 693)

Very little is known about the two intermediate authors Vajraghaṇṭā (A.D. 681) and Kacchapā (A.D. 693), because we have practically no historical information regarding their birthplace or their biography. Padmavajra, who comes next, was a great name in Tāntric Buddhism, and stands first in the first succession list given above. He was an author of a large number of works, out of which only two are extant in Sanskrit, while many others are preserved in translations in the Tibetan Tangyur. According to Tāranātha, he was the first to introduce the *Hevajratantra* in Vajrayāna, which he did along with his collaborator, Kambalapāda. Tāranātha also makes Padmavajra a contemporary of Indrabhūti, Lalitavajra and Kukkuripā.[3] This Lalitavajra is said to have introduced the three divisions of the *Kṛṣṇayamāritantra*,[4] and, therefore, should be distinguished from the later Lalitagupta, who was a disciple of Advayavajra. Kukkuripā, another contemporary of his, is believed to have introduced into Vajrayāna the *Mahāmāyātantra*.

Padmavajra was a historical figure, and a very interesting

[1] op. cit., 2e partie, p. 33.

[2] *Pag Sam Jon Zan*, index, p. cxv.

[3] *Tāranātha*, p. 188.

[4] *Tāranātha*, p. 275 f.

work of his, entitled the *Guhyasiddhi*,[1] has lately been discovered. This was considered a work of great authority in Tibet, even so late as A.D. 1747, when the *Pag Sam Jon Zan* was written. The whole work is written in what is called the twilight language, or the 'Sandhyābhāṣā'; but there is enough to show to an ordinary reader that he advocated many mystic and objectionable rites and practices, which he termed secret rites. According to Padmavajra, such practices and rites were first formulated by the Buddha, and were recorded in the 'Śrīsamāja', which is only another name of the *Guhyasamājatantra*. He says there is no better treasure in the three worlds than the Śrīsamāja. He further says how wonderful are the teachings of Vajrayāna, which are the most secret of all secrets and are without Svabhāva (real nature) and are pure and incomparable! He advocates the meditation on the Prajñā (the wisdom) and the Upāya (the means) and the remembrance of the adamantine mind, all of which are more secret than all secrets, and which are not possible of attainment without the female element, or the Śakti. He asks his followers to enjoy the Mahāmudrā conjoined with the Upāya, which is in their own bodies, and says that the knowledge of Mahāmudrā is most auspicious and of a very peculiar nature, which can be realized by one's own self only. Padmavajra, in accordance with the teachings of the *Guhyasamāja*, follows the doctrine of the five Dhyāni Buddhas, and says that by these five forms alone Sambodhi can be attained in accordance with the pronouncement of the Tathāgatas. Siddhi, or perfection, is indeed difficult of attainment in one life; but those who so desire should, according to Padmavajra, take up the secret rite, which is the destroyer of all thoughts of duality. If he is initiated in the Tantra of Śrīsamāja, which is the cause of all happiness, he may attain divine perfection by coming in contact with the Mahāmudrā (or the great woman). But in order

[1] MS. copies exist in the Oriental Institute, Baroda, and the library of Mm. Haraprasād Śāstrī.

to do so the initiation (Abhiṣeka) must be taken from a guru, without whose kind assistance no success can follow. Throughout the *Guhyasiddhi* similar ideas occur, and it is not necessary to enumerate the practices inculcated therein. The long and short of the whole work is, that without Mahāmudrā no emancipation or success in any rite is possible.[1] But if the worshipper is initiated into the Mahāmudrā cult, success is assured even if he may do things which are against all laws, social or religious.[2]

6. JĀLANDHARIPĀ (A.D. 705)

Jālandharipā, also known as Hāḍipā, whom we have placed one generation after Padmavajra, or Saroruhavajra, is made by Tāranātha[3] a contemporary of several important personalities, such as Bhartṛhari, Vimalacandra, Kṛṣṇācārya, Tāntipā and even Dharmakīrti. In the *Pag Sam Jon Zan*[4] it is recorded that he was buried in a hole underground, by the order of the king Gopicandra of Cāṭigāon, who was afterwards converted to mysticism by the Ācārya. It is, indeed, very difficult to place him correctly from the above accounts, and all that can be said now is that Jālandharipā was regarded as a very ancient Siddhācārya, as may be evidenced by Tāranātha's making him a contemporary of Dharmakīrti, whose time is definitely known to be the first half of the seventh century A.D. His other contemporaries are mostly mysterious persons, and none can say with any measure of accuracy as to the time when they flourished. The very fact that Jālandharipā wrote a commentary on a work of Saroruhavajra[5] and followed the *Hevajratantra* introduced by him,[6] places him one

[1] महामुद्रां निषेवेत स्वदेहोपायसंयुताम् । स्वसंवेद्या हि सा विद्या महामुद्रा परा शुभा ॥

[2] येन येन हि बध्यन्ते जन्तवो रौद्रकर्मणा । सोपायेन तु तेनैव मुच्यन्ते भवबन्धनात् ॥

[3] op. cit., p. 195.

[4] op. cit., index, p. xcvii. The same story is repeated in many old Bengali works.

[5] *Catalogue du Fonds Tibétain*, 2e partie, p. 18.

[6] *Tāranātha*, p. 275 f.

generation after Padmavajra, who flourished at the end of the seventh century.

A very interesting story is recorded of the life of Hāḍipā, or Jālandharipā, more or less in the same strain in a number of old Bengali books, such as the *Dharmamaṅgala*, *Śūnyapurāṇa*, *Mānikcānder Gān*, *Mayanāmatir Gān*, *Gopicānder Gīt*, *Gopicānder Sannyās*, etc. In all these stories Hāḍipā is connected with several other important personages, viz. the queen Mayanāmatī, her husband, the king Mānikcandra of the sixteen Vaṅgas, Gopicandra, their only son, and Kṛṣṇācārya, or Kānhupā, one of Hāḍipā's disciples. It is recorded that when Gopicandra was born, the royal guru had predicted that he would not live for more than 19 years. This fact was known only to the queen, who used to pass all her time in meditation, and was nicknamed by her husband the king, Muni, or the ascetic. When Gopicandra was only a boy of twelve, his father, without giving intimation to his wife, married him to four princesses, namely Phandanā, Candanā, Rodanā and Padunā. Soon after this marriage king Mānikcandra died of fever. Mayanāmatī thereafter became very anxious, on account of the possibility of her son's meeting with a premature death. In order that this calamity might be averted, she persuaded her son to take initiation from Hāḍipā who was a Siddha, but unluckily the rāja could not remember the mantras, and, once being unable to fill miraculously with water a dried up tank by the incantation of the mantra taught by Hāḍipā, he became enraged and buried the sage underneath the stable.

For a long time Hāḍipā's disciple, Kṛṣṇācārya, or popularly known as Kānhupā, made a search for his guru and became anxious at his sudden and mysterious disappearance. But later on, however, he came to know about the whereabouts of Hāḍipā by mystic means, and went straight to Mayanāmatī and told her about the foolish actions of her son, Gopicandra. In order, however, to protect Gopicandra from the anger of Hāḍipā, they both hit upon the device of placing a golden image of Gopicandra in front of the hole in which Hāḍipā was buried underground. They removed the earth, and as soon as the body of the guru was seen all those present prostrated themselves on the earth; but, as the image did not show any respect, Hāḍipā became enraged and through his anger the image melted and was turned into ashes. Mayanāmatī at this opportunity held a bagful of Indian hemp before the guru, who had been by this time in Samādhi for full five years. He broke his fast with a maund and a quarter of hemp, the same quantity of Kucila (nux vomica), and Dhaturā (stramonium). But ultimately he understood the whole trick played upon him by Kānhupā, and pronounced a curse that he would be beheaded at the fort of Ḍāhukā.

The queen, Mayanāmatī, again persuaded Hāḍipā to give initiation to Gopicandra so that his premature death might be averted. Gopicandra at first was very obstinate, but ultimately yielded. The queens of Gopicandra scented danger, and wanted to dispose of Hāḍipā by means of poison, but he passed through the ordeal entirely unharmed. Ultimately Gopicandra took the initiation and Hāḍipā put him to a severe test for twelve long years, after which he obtained perfection.[1]

7. ANAṄGAVAJRA (A.D. 705)

Anaṅgavajra, the disciple of Padmavajra, is characterized in the history of the eighty-four Siddhapuruṣas as the son of king Gopāla of Eastern India. The time of Gopāla has been fixed by V. A. Smith as *cir.* A.D. 730–40.[2] But S. C. Vidyābhūṣaṇa places him between A.D. 695 and 705.[3] Dr. S. Kṛṣṇaswāmi Iyengar doubts the date of V. A. Smith; and, in the absence of any inscriptional or monumental evidence, we are in favour of accepting the

[1] See, for instance, *Gopicānder Sannyās*, ed. N. K. Bhaṭṭaśālī, intro., p. 11 f.

[2] *E.H.I.*, 3rd edition, p. 397.

[3] *History of Indian Logic*, p. 323.

earlier date.[1] Anaṅgavajra's date will, therefore, be in consonance with the theory advanced in the history of the eighty-four Mahāsiddhas. Anaṅgavajra seems to be a fairly well known author, as can be seen from the number of works written by him, the translations of which now find place in the Tibetan Tangyur. One of his famous compositions is the *Prajñopāyaviniścayasiddhi*, and the work is characterized by its boldness of spirit, its lucidity of teaching and brevity of expression. This work has now been published as No. XLIV of the Gaekwad's Oriental Series, as one of the *Two Vajrayāna Works*. Like Jālandharipā, who was probably his contemporary, he also composed several works on the *Hevajratantra*, which was for the first time introduced into Buddhism by his preceptor, Padmavajra.

8. INDRABHŪTI (A.D. 717)

Indrabhūti, the next author of importance, was the king of Uḍḍiyāna, which is generally identified with Orissa but which may also quite conceivably be a part of Bengal.[2] He was the father of Padmasambhava, who, conjointly with the famous logician, Śāntarakṣita, erected the first regular monastery at Samye, in Tibet, in the year A.D. 749.[3] Indrabhūti's sister was Lakṣmīṅkarā, who was married, according to the history of the eighty-four Siddhas,[4] to the prince of Sambhala, the counterpart of Uḍḍiyāna, and attained Siddhi. He was regarded as an authority on Vajrayāna and Tantra long after his time.[5] He has written a large number of works and at least twenty-three among them are

[1] It is quite possible that he ruled during the years named by V. A. Smith, but it is very likely that he ascended the throne by popular consent at a very late age.

[2] See supra, chap. V, pp. 44–46.

[3] Waddell, *Lamaism*, p. 576.

[4] *Die Geschisten der 84 Zanberer;* see *Indrabhūti.*

[5] H. P. Śāstrī, *Nepal Catalogue*, Vol. II, p. 56.

preserved in the pages of the Tibetan Tangyur translations.[1] We have, however, been fortunate in discovering at least two of his works in original Sanskrit; namely, the *Kurukullā-sādhana*,[2] which appears in the *Sādhanamālā*, and the *Jñānasiddhi*. This latter has been published along with the work of Anaṅgavajra as No. XLIV in the Gaekwad's Oriental Series. The *Jñānasiddhi* is an extremely interesting work in twenty-two chapters, giving in a nutshell many leading doctrines and rites of Vajrayāna, which throw immense light on this obscure religion.

9. KṚṢṆĀCĀRYA (A.D. 717)

The next author in chronological order is Kṛṣṇācārya. In the Tangyur[3] several Kṛṣṇācāryas are found, and it is indeed difficult to differentiate between them in the absence of more definite materials. Tārānātha makes Kṛṣṇācārya a contemporary of Jālandhari, Bhartṛhari, Gopicandra and even Dharmakīrti. But he is probably wrong in making him a contemporary of Dharmakīrti, who is definitely known to have flourished in the first half of the seventh century. Kṛṣṇācārya seems to be a contemporary of Jālandhari and Gopicandra,[4] both of whom in all probability flourished in the first quarter of the eighth century. According to the *Pag Sam Jon Zan*, this Kṛṣṇa was born of a Brāhmaṇ family of Orissa, and was initiated into the mystic cult by Jālandharipā. Kṛṣṇa had a disciple in Tāntipā,[5] who was a weaver. Kṛṣṇa is credited in the same work with having introduced the Tantras in which the male and female divinities sit clasping each other.[6] Kṛṣṇācārya wrote Dohās also in his own vernacular, which was probably Uḍiyā and had a great affinity with the old Bengali language. No less than 12 songs of his are available in the

[1] *Bauddha Gān O Dohā*, app., p. 14. [2] op. cit., p. 353.

[3] *Bauddha Gān O Dohā*, app., pp. 21 ff.

[4] Sukur Muhammad, *Gopicānder Sannyās*, intro., p. 2.

[5] op. cit., index, p. v. [6] op. cit., p. lvii.

original vernacular, and were printed and published for the first time in the *Bauddha Gān O Dohā*.[1]

10. LAKṢMĪṄKARĀ (A.D. 729)

In the history of Vajrayāna the name of Bhagavatī Lakṣmī, or Lakṣmīṅkarā, is interesting, not only because she was a woman, but also because of the novel doctrines she preached without reserve and with great confidence and emphasis. Born in the royal family of Uḍḍiyāna, a sister of Indrabhūti, she showed remarkable boldness in preaching her own peculiar theories in a short but interesting work, entitled the *Advayasiddhi*.[2] This work was long lost in the original Sanskrit, but was preserved in the Tibetan Tangyur in translation.[3] To this work the attention of scholars was first drawn by Dr. Mm. Haraprasād Śāstrī, in an article contributed to one of the stray numbers of the *Dacca Review*. We have since had an opportunity of studying this book more carefully, and the leading ideas revealed by its study are summarized below. Throughout this work, the influence of Indrabhūti's *Jñānasiddhi* is very perceptible; and this is due probably to the fact that Lakṣmīṅkarā was not only a sister of Indrabhūti, but also one of his favourite disciples.[4]

In the *Advayasiddhi* a most remarkable and bold innovation is introduced by the authoress. Hitherto the Vajrayānists advocated the worship of the five Dhyāni Buddhas and their innumerable emanations; but what Lakṣmīṅkarā advocated was quite unusual and strange, even though since her time this new teaching gradually won many adherents, who were styled Sahajiyās; and are still to be found among the Nāḍhā Nāḍhīs of Bengal, and especially among the Bāuls. Lakṣmīṅkarā declares

[1] See, for instance, op. cit., p. 18.

[2] Copies of the MS. are available in the libraries of the Oriental Institute, Baroda, and Mm. Haraprasād Śāstrī.

[3] op. cit., 2e partie, p. 211.

[4] ibid., p. 211.

that no suffering, no fasting, no rites, no bathing, no purification nor other rules of society are necessary; nor do you need to bow down before the images of gods, which are prepared of wood, stone or mud; but you should with concentration offer worship to your own body, where all gods reside.[1]

She explains later on, without however openly declaring the truth, that when the truth is known there is no restriction for the worshipper. He can eat anything, he can drink anything and violate any laws, human or divine. Towards women, she declares, no hatred should be displayed; because they are the embodiments of the Prajñā in restraint.[2] Later on, she says that instructions on Nirvāṇa should always be obtained from the preceptor. In the whole of the movable and immovable world, there is nothing better than the guru, through whose kind offices the wise obtain many kinds of perfection.[3]

11. LĪLĀVAJRA (A.D. 741)

Lakṣmīṅkarā's direct disciple was Līlāvajra.[4] He had also a great reputation as a Vajrācārya, and wrote a large number of authoritative works. So far as we know, none of his works is extant in the original Sanskrit, though many are preserved in translations in the pages of the Tibetan Tangyur.[5] No less than nine works of his are mentioned in the Tangyur Catalogue, and, from their titles, it can be surmised that both Vajrayāna and Sahajayāna were in a flourishing condition in his time; and that the *Guhyasamājatantra* and the *Kṛṣṇaya-*

[1] न कष्टकल्पनां कुर्यात् नोपवासो न च क्रियाम् । स्नानं शौचं न चैवात्र ग्रामधर्मविवर्जनम् ॥ न चापि वन्दयेद्देवान् काष्टपाषाणमृण्मयान् । पूजामस्यैव कायस्य कुर्यान्नित्यं समाहितः ॥

[2] गम्यागम्यविकल्पं तु भक्ष्याभक्ष्यं तथैव च । पेयापेयं तथा मन्त्री कुर्यान्नैव समाहितः ॥ सर्ववर्णसमुद्भूता जुगुप्सा नैव योषितः । सैव भगवती प्रज्ञा सम्वृत्या रूपमाश्रिता ॥

[3] आचार्यात् परतरं नास्ति त्रैलोक्ये सचराचरे । यस्य प्रसादात् प्राप्यन्ते सिद्धयोऽनेकधा बुधैः ॥

[4] *Catalogue du Fonds Tibêtain*, 2e partie, p. 212.

[5] *Bauddha Gān O Dohā*, app., p. 75.

māritantra were regarded as works of very great authority. It appears from the Tangyur that he acknowledged another guru, by name Vilāsavajra,[1] besides Lakṣmīṅkarā already mentioned. In the same way, besides Dārikapāda he had another devoted disciple, who called himself Karuṇācala. This latter was a poet of a very high order, and several of his compositions are published in the *Sādhanamālā*.[2] His verses are distinguished by an easy flowing diction and devotional language. At the end of the Sādhana of the Vajramahākāla he has respectfully mentioned the name of his guru, Līlāvajra.

12. DĀRIKAPĀDA (A.D. 753)

The name of Dārikapāda, one of the disciples of Līlāvajra,[3] is fairly well known through the publication of the *Bauddha Gān O Dohā*. From this work it is evident that Dārika belonged to Bengal and wrote a number of songs in his vernacular, some of which are recorded in the work above referred to.[4] In one of his songs he offers his obeisance to Luipā,[5] and this leads the editor, Dr. Mm. Śāstrī, to think that Dārika was a direct disciple of Lui.[6] It has already been shown that Luipā belonged to an earlier age, and so any close connexion between the two is hardly admissible. Dārika probably mentioned Lui because Lui is regarded in some quarters as the first Siddhācārya, and this seems to be a more reasonable explanation. Dārika composed a pretty large number of works in Sanskrit; but none of them is now extant in the original. At least ten works of his are preserved in translations in the Tibetan Tangyur,[7] where Dārika is credited with having written books on the *Cakrasamvaratantra*, *Kālacakratantra* and *Vajrayoginītantra*.

[1] *Catalogue du Fonds Tibétain*, 2e partie, p. 87.

[2] op. cit., p. 590, also 391 (Līlāśani) लीलावज्रगुरो: प्रणम्य चरणं, etc.

[3] *Catalogue du Fonds Tibétain*, 2e partie, p. 212.

[4] op. cit., intro., p. 30.

[5] op. cit., p. 53, लुइ पाअपए, etc.

[6] op. cit., intro., p. 30.

[7] *Bauddha Gān O Dohā*, index, pp. 39, 40.

13. SAHAJAYOGINĪ CINTĀ (A.D. 765)

Next comes Sahajayoginī Cintā, a female ascetic and a disciple of Dārikapāda, who is known to us as the authoress of the *Vyaktabhāvānugatatattvasiddhi*.[1] A translation of this in Tibetan also exists.[2] It appears from her work that she was a follower of the Vijñānavādin school, and laid particular stress on the universe being nothing but the creation of the Citta, or mind. It is the mind, she says, which begets miseries, and in consequence creates external objects. The Prajñā and Upāya are also creations of the mind, and when they combine they give rise to Mahāsukha in the mind, which fancies the whole external world to be the forms of Mahāsukha. The mind, she says, has its vagaries and its own ways: sometimes it is sleeping, sometimes it is awake, sometimes it begets desires, sometimes it is pure and at others it is impure, sometimes it has many forms, and sometimes it is in an indescribable state. The Yogin, who is able to realize the voidness of the external world and keep his mind free from reflections in all its different states and in all its vagaries and ways, is really the emancipated; and Buddha-hood for him is easy of attainment. At the end of the work, the authoress describes Vajrasattva in eloquent language, and pays him a glowing tribute by characterizing him as one who is realized by self alone, who defies comparison and is omnipresent and all-pervading, who is the creator, destroyer and protector of the universe, and who brings into prominence the manifestations of the mind.[3]

14. ḌOMBĪ HERUKA (A.D. 777)

Next comes Ḍombī Heruka, the disciple of Sahajayoginī, who, like Dārika, is well known to many through the publication

[1] A copy of the MS. is preserved in the Oriental Institute, Baroda.

[2] *Bauddha Gān O Dohā*, app., p. 96.

[3] प्रत्यात्मवेद्यो भगवान् उपमावर्जितः प्रभुः । सर्वगः सर्वव्यापी च कर्ता हर्ता जगत्पतिः । श्रीमान् वज्रसत्वोऽसौ व्यक्तभावप्रकाशकः ॥

of the *Bauddha Gān O Dohā* already referred to. The Tibetan authorities agree in recording that he was a king of Magadha, but became an ascetic later on.[1] In the Tibetan Tangyur he is designated as Ācārya, Mahācārya and Siddhācārya, and his name is included in the list of the eighty-four Mahāsiddhas. He wrote books on Sahajayāna and Vajrayāna, and composed a book of songs in vernacular entitled the *Ḍombī-gītikā*. Several of his songs are recorded in the *Bauddha Gān O Dohā*, and very probably they are taken from this *Ḍombī-gītikā* composed by him. He composed a Sādhana of the goddess, Nairātmā, and this is recorded in the *Sādhanamālā*.[2] It appears from the very opening lines of this Sādhana that he followed the *Hevajratantra*.[3] He wrote a fairly large number of works in Sanskrit, and among them at least eight are extant in translations in the Tibetan Tangyur.[4] Besides these eight, he wrote another work entitled the *Sahajasiddhi*,[5] which has been discovered in the original Sanskrit. This is a highly interesting work, even though it is short and divided into three small chapters, not exceeding a hundred verses in all. In it there are certain topics of absorbing interest, and we take this opportunity of recording some of the views expressed by the author.

Ḍombī formulates that the worship of Kula is the most important in the Tāntric religion; without it no success can be achieved; but with it great success is possible of attainment.[6] While explaining the word, Kula, he says, Kulas are five in number and they originate from the five Dhyāni Buddhas, Akṣobhya, Vairocana, Amitābha, Ratnasambhava and Amoghasiddhi; and

[1] *Tārānātha*, p. 323; *Pag Sam Jon Zan*, index, p. cxliii.

[2] op. cit., p. 443.

[3] डोम्बीहेरुकपादैर्देवीचक्रस्य भावना कथिता । सञ्चिन्त्य सकल तत्त्वं हेवज्रात् योगिनीतन्त्रात् ॥

[4] *Bauddha Gān*, app., p. 34.

[5] A copy is preserved in the Oriental Institute, Baroda.

[6] कुलसेवात् भवेत् सिध्दिः सर्वकामप्रदा शुभा ।

this is the reason why they are called Kuleśas, or the lords of the Kulas or the families. Ḍombī thus echoes the doctrines inculcated in the *Guhyasamāja*, the earliest Vajrayāna work extant.

From the word Kula, the words Kulācāra, Kuladharma, Kaula, Kaulika, etc., are derived. The Kaulas declare themselves to be Tāntric Hindus. From the literature extant on Kaulism, the meaning of Kula is not clear. Moreover, the large number of interpretations of the word shows unmistakably that the Hindus were not certain about the meaning of it; but the meaning in the Buddhist sense, as expressed in the *Guhyasamāja* and the *Sahajasiddhi*, is quite clear and unequivocal. The Buddhists gave only a single interpretation of the word; the Kaulas, according to them, mean the worshippers or the followers of the originators of the five families, namely of the five Dhyāni Buddhas. The question will then arise as to whether the Kaulas are really Hindu or Buddhist in origin. We cannot here discuss this great question, which should remain open for the present until sufficient materials are at hand to prove either theory. There is, however, very little difference between the Kulācāra of the Hindus and the Tāntric practices of the Buddhists; because in both the desire to do improper and illegal things to the fullest extent is present.

Ḍombī Heruka has explained Mahāsukha; and the happiness obtainable from it has been fully dealt with. Happiness, which can best be obtained from one's own experience, according to him, has four successive stages: Ānanda, Paramānanda, Viramānanda and Sahajānanda. By the combination of the two elements, Prajñā and Upāya, these four stages of great happiness can be obtained.[1] It can only be experienced by one's own self, and when it is realized emancipation, or perfection, can easily be attained. In

[1] आनन्देन सुखं किञ्चित् परमानन्दस्ततोऽधिकम् ।
विरमानन्दो विरामः स्यात् सहजानन्दस्तु शेषतः ॥

the eleventh century Advayavajra also voiced the same opinion.[1] Ḍombī Heruka was also responsible for introducing certain new elements which are not mentioned here, as that would be going into minute details unnecessarily.

The next period of the development of Tāntric culture among the Buddhists is represented by a set of most powerful writers and popular gurus, such as Dīpaṅkara (A.D. 980–1053), Advayavajra, or Avadhūtipā, his disciple, Lalitavajra,[2] Tailopā of Cāṭigāon (Chittagong), Ratnākaraśānti, Prajñākaramati and Nāropā, all of whom were contemporaries of king Mahīpāla I of the Pāla dynasty,[3] who flourished between A.D. 978 and 1030. Those who are interested in this latest development of the Tāntric culture of the Buddhists, are recommended to consult the excellent edition of the *Advayavajrasaṁgraha*, which is published, with a summary and a scholarly introduction in English, by Dr. Mm. Haraprasād Śāstrī, the celebrated authority on the subject, in the Gaekwad's Oriental Series as No. XL.

[1] *Advayavajrasaṁgraha* (G.O.S., No. 40), p. 32.

[2] cf. *Sādhanamālā*, p. 267.

श्रीमदद्वयवज्रस्य गुरोर्नत्वा पदाम्बुजम् । श्रीमल्ललितगुप्तेन तारासाधनमुच्यते ॥

[3] *Indian Teachers of Buddhist Universities*, p. 158.

CHAPTER IX

AIMS AND OBJECTS

THE aims and objects of the Tāntrics, as has been indicated already, were either to obtain emancipation or the countless Siddhis, or perfections, mostly for prosperity and happiness in the present life. The word Siddhi is closely associated with the word Sādhana, which means a procedure by which one can attain the different perfections. The *Sādhanamālā* of the Buddhists consists of three hundred and twelve such Sādhanas, indicating the methods to be pursued for obtaining particular Siddhis. The worshipper should always take care to conform to the directions given in the Sādhana and to practise the rites with patience and zeal. The Hindus generally recognize eight Siddhis, though occasionally 18 and 24 Siddhis are also acknowledged. The eight Siddhis[1] are:

अणिमा	Atomization.
लघिमा	Levitation.
महिमा	Magnification.
प्राप्ति	Extension.
प्राकाम्य	Efficacy.
ईशित्व	Sovereignty.
वशित्व	Mastery (over elements).
कामावसायित्व	Capacity to will actual facts.

In the *Brahmavaivartapurāṇa*[2] mention is made of 34 kinds of Siddhis; including the eight already cited. Some of them are:

[1] *Patañjali Yogasūtra*, III, 45; and its commentary.

[2] *Kṛṣṇajanmakhaṇḍa*, chap. 78, śl. 20–29. See also *Tantrasāra* (Vasumatī, 5th ed.), p. 417.

दूरश्रवण	Power to hear distant sounds.
परकायप्रवेशन	Power to enter into other people's bodies.
मनोयायित्व	Power to go at will.
सर्वज्ञत्व	Omniscience.
वह्निस्तम्भ	Power to stop the progress of fire.
जलस्तम्भ	Power to stop the current of water.
चिरजीवित्व	Immortality.
वायुस्तम्भ	Power to stop the current of air.
क्षुत्पिपासानिद्रास्तम्भ	Full control over hunger, thirst and sleep.
कायव्यूहप्रवेश	Entering into all kinds of physical bodies.
वाक्सिध्दि	Perfection in speech.
मृतानयन	Power to revive the dead.
प्राणाकर्षण	Power to draw vital force.
प्राणदान	Power to award life.
इन्द्रियस्तम्भ	Power to stop the functions of the sense organs.
बुध्दिस्तम्भ	Power to deaden the intellect.

One who is able to attain, by a particular process, a large number of the foregoing powers is called a Siddhapuruṣa, or one who has attained perfection. In mediæval times, it is said there were many Siddhapuruṣas in India, who surprised people by their wonderful, miraculous and stupendous feats. The Buddhists recognized 84 such Siddhapuruṣas, and in Nepal and Tibet homage is still paid to their memory. They are venerated in these countries, and their traditional likenesses are still found hanging on the temple walls and other places.

The Siddhas again are of three varieties, according to the *Tantrasāra*, a Hindu Tāntric work, composed by Kṛṣṇānanda Āgamavāgīśa, who flourished in about the seventeenth century of the Christian era. The three varieties are:[1] Uttama or the first class, Madhyama or the middle, and Adhama or the lowest class, and the characteristics of each class are also enumerated in the

[1] *Tantrasāra*, op. cit., p. 417.

same treatise. According to it, a Siddha will be recognized as belonging to the first class, when he is able to fulfil all his desires by mere thought, or, in other words, as soon as a desire arises in his mind that very moment it is fulfilled. The second class of Siddhas is able to conquer death, commune with gods, enter unperceived into the bodies and homes of others, move in the firmament, hear the gods conversing in the heavens, understand all terrestrial truths, obtain ornaments, conveyances, etc., enjoy long life, bewitch people, perform miracles, remove diseases by a mere glance, extract poison, obtain erudition in all branches of knowledge, renounce all worldly enjoyments, practise Yoga in all its eight sub-divisions, show compassion to all beings, obtain omniscience, etc. The third or lowest class of Siddhas obtains fame, long-life, conveyances, ornaments, familiarity with the king, popularity with royal personages and the people, power to bewitch, wealth and prosperity, children and family.

It can be easily seen from the above that the Siddhas belonging to the third class were never designated as Siddhapuruṣas, who were attached either to the first class or the middle class. In all Tantras, Hindu or Buddhist, general directions are always given as to the manner of obtaining Siddhi by the muttering of mantras. In case legitimate muttering of the mantras and conformity to the regulations do not bestow the desired Siddhi, the Tantras also give directions for obtaining it by seven different processes.[1]

Having thus described the nature of the Siddhas or magicians, let us now proceed to characterize the different Siddhis or perfections, the possession of one or the other of which entitles a man to be called a magician. The word, Siddhi, may be defined as the attainment of super-normal powers of the mind, body or the sense-organs. The Siddhi is generally known to be of five

[1] *Tantrasāra*, op. cit., p. 415 : उपायास्तत्र कर्तव्याः सप्त शङ्करभाषिताः ।

varieties[1]—Janmaja (co-existent with birth), Auṣadhija (due to drug), Mantraja (due to the agency of mystic syllables), Tapoja (due to austerities), and Samādhija (by reason of intense meditation). The mind is compared to a river in the rainy season, with all the exits closed except one, through which the water rushes with tremendous vigour. When the mind in the same way is concentrated on one particular thought, and is not allowed to wander away through numberless channels, it is able to acquire great strength, which is called Siddhi, or perfection.

Siddhis, as conceived by the Buddhist Tāntrics, are of various kinds, and range from success in love affairs to the attainment of the highest emancipation, and they owe their origin mostly to mantras or magic syllables. If we examine the kind of Siddhis for the attainment of which the Buddhists of the Tāntric age busied themselves in muttering mantras and executing complicated Tāntric practices, we shall be able to understand the aims and objects of the people and their mentality. Hence, a study of these practices is not superfluous, as it is capable of throwing a flood of light on the state of Tāntric culture among the Buddhists.

In all Tāntric works of the Buddhists great anxiety is shown for averting and curing diseases, and for the extraction of snake poison and prevention of snake-bites. This is quite natural, because these matters are practically beyond human control, and, therefore, the aid of magic was eagerly sought by the afflicted people. Next in importance to the above is the longing for acquiring a knowledge of the Śāstras without their study, but only through the agency of mantras. They also believed that Bodhi, or emancipation, was obtainable through the agency of mantras alone, or when mantras were associated with certain practices. Great anxiety is also shown for the attainment of Sarvajñattva, or omniscience, or the position of a Buddha, both

[1] *Patañjali Yogasūtra*, I, 1.

signifying one and the same thing, namely emancipation. The six cruel rites and the eight great Siddhis also had their share of attention. The Tāntric Buddhists also possessed a great desire to have the mighty Hindu gods as their servants, whom they believed to be conquerable by mantras and willing to do menial work for the magician.

They also believed that the benign act of protection could be granted by divine agencies and also secured by mantras. Curiously enough, the aid of mantras was widely availed of by the Tāntric Buddhists for vanquishing their opponents in public discussions.[1] From this it appears clear that religious discussions in public assemblies were very common, and victory in these assemblies was eagerly sought by all classes of people, including the Buddhists; and it is no wonder that gods and mantras should be invented in order that the Sādhaka might easily obtain victory in learned assemblies without being qualified for it. This leads us to believe in the stories recorded in the *Pag Sam Jon Zan*, that in public assemblies disputants of various religions used to assemble and take part, each staking his own religion. Thus people were converted and re-converted to different religious systems when defeated in public discussions, sometimes with a large retinue of their disciples. Those who claim in modern days that the Hindus in earlier days never made converts belonging to other religions are, therefore, not quite correct in their information.

A great desire is also shown to perform miracles, probably for the purpose of creating an impression on the public mind as to the benefits accruing from the practices enjoined in the Tantras. Whether or not they could actually obtain such spiritual powers as they claimed, it is not the province of this treatise to discuss. But

[1] cf. Sādhanas in the *Sādhanamālā*, No. 151: यस्यां भावितमात्रायां निग्रहः सर्ववादिनाम्, No. 155: यस्योदयेन निद्राति वादिनां मुखपङ्कजम्, No. 218: पर्षदनभिभवनीयो वादी, No. 256: सर्वत्र वादे विजयिता । etc.

we read in the Tantras the story of monks who were habituated to go out for alms, as is evident from the devices invented by them which miraculously induced people to offer alms of their own accord.[1]

Their conception of future happiness was also of an interesting character. In one place a desire is expressed for a Siddhi which will enable the worshipper to remain in a state of rapture in the company of numberless Apsarasas in the land of the Vidyādharas, where the Lord of Heaven will hold the parasol over his head, Brahmā will act as the prime minister, Vemacitrī as the army-commander, Hari as the gate-keeper, and the naked god, Śaṅkara, will discourse on the different virtues.[2] The monks usually led a poor life; but they were, nevertheless, anxious for wealth, and believed that wealth could be obtained by the muttering of mantras alone. Jambhala, the god of wealth, was created by them; several forms of his were conceived by them, a large number of mantras were invented and a number of Sādhanas were devoted to his worship. These, and similar instances, are evidence of the attraction wealth had for the poor monks.

The Buddhists also acknowledged eight great Siddhis, though they were somewhat different from the eight Siddhis acknowledged by the Hindus. According to the Buddhists, the eight Siddhis are: (1) Khaḍga, (2) Añjana, (3) Pādalepa, (4) Antardhāna, (5) Rasarasāyana, (6) Khecara, (7) Bhūcara, (8) Pātāla.[3]

It is difficult to get an explanation of these Siddhis correctly from any Buddhist work; but evidently the first, Khaḍga,

[1] Sādhana, No. 235: ततः सिन्दूरेण नन्द्यावर्ताकृतितिलकं विधाय ग्रामं प्रविशेत् । यत्र तत् तिलकं संक्रान्तं दृश्यते तं यत्नेनाराधयेत् ॥

[2] Sādhana, No. 260: अनेकाभिरप्सरोभिः परिवृतः पुरस्कृतः विद्याधरस्थाने बहलसुखमनुभवन् एव तिष्ठति, देवेन्द्रः छत्रधरो भवति, ब्रह्मा च मन्त्री, वैमचित्री सैन्यपतिः हरिः प्रतिहारः . . . नग्नाचार्यः शङ्करः समस्तगुणानुपदर्शयति ।

[3] *Sādhanamālā*, p. 350: खड्गाञ्जनपादलेपान्तर्धानरसरसायनखेचरभूचरपातालसिध्दिप्रमुखाः सिध्दीः साधयेत् ॥

signifies the perfection which enables a person to conquer in battle with the help of a sword over which mantras have been muttered. The second, Añjana, very probably refers to the magic unguent which, when applied to the eyes, enables a person to perceive the treasures buried under the earth, or otherwise hidden from the eyes. The third, Pādalepa, refers to the mysterious ointment which, when applied to the feet, enables a person to move about everywhere without his body being perceived by any one. The fourth, Antardhāna, similarly refers to the mysterious power which enables a person to disappear miraculously before the very eyes of the people watching him. The fifth, Rasarasāyana, refers probably either to the magic solution which turns baser metals into gold, or the medicine which gives immunity from death. The sixth, Khecara, enables one to move in the firmament. The seventh, Bhūcara, gives a person power to go at will anywhere on this earth in a moment; and the eighth, Pātāla, refers to the power of going to the nether-worlds. Such feats were considered superhuman, and the monks of the Tāntric age directed their attention to executing such superhuman feats through the agency of mantras, which they thought helped to develop psychic power.

The most important among the different rites of the Tāntrics are probably what are known as the Ṣaṭkarma, or the six rites, and it is necessary here to give some idea of the different rites with which the old monks always busied themselves. These six rites are: Śānti, Vaśīkaraṇa, Stambhana, Vidveṣaṇa, Uccāṭana and Māraṇa. The first, Śānti, is a rite which is calculated to remove diseases and save persons from the terrible consequences of evil stars or of bad actions done in previous births. The second, Vaśīkaraṇa, is the rite which gives the performer the power to bewitch all other men or women, or even gods and animals, and get work done by them. The third, Stambhana, is the rite by the performance of which power is conferred on the worshipper for stopping all actions of others, and to stop the effect even when its cause is operating. Thus the burning power of fire can be stopped, so that even when fire is present it will not burn. It is the rite by which all actions of human beings can be stopped at will. The fourth, Vidveṣaṇa, is another interesting rite which gives the performer the power to separate two friends, relatives, lovers, and so forth, from each other, and the power to create animosity between two friends. The fifth, Uccāṭana, is the rite which when performed gives the performer special power to make his enemy flee from the country, with all attendant disgrace. Uccāṭana was also employed in destroying the dwelling-houses of enemies by incantations of mantras and other means. The sixth, Māraṇa, is perhaps the most cruel among the six cruel rites of Tāntrism. This consists in killing, or permanently injuring, enemies by means of apparently harmless practices.

These are known as Ṣaṭkarmas, and it is said that experienced Tāntrics, even in modern times, get results immediately these rites are performed. It is, nevertheless, difficult for ordinary laymen to obtain any successful result, because the rites have to be performed according to time, planets, seasons, gods and mantras appropriate to the rite, which are known only to the specialists. The mantras are of primary importance in all cruel rites, and no less than six methods of application are generally formulated: (1) Grathana—consists in reciting the mantra over each of the letters of the name of the medium[1] (Sādhya): generally required in Śānti (protective rites). (2) Vidarbha—consists in reciting the letters on the name of the medium between the letters of the mantra: used mostly in Vaśīkaraṇa, or bewitching. (3) Sampuṭa—consists in reciting the mantra both in the beginning and at the end of the name of the medium: mostly required in Stambhana. (4) Rodhana—

[1] This word is purposely used to denote the object which is to be conquered or benefited, as the case may be. The best word from modern Spiritualism which may stand for Sādhya is the word 'medium'.

consists in applying the mantra in the beginning, middle and at the end of the name of the medium: required in Vidveṣaṇa. (5) Yoga—consists in reciting the name of the medium at the end of the mantra: required in Uccāṭana. (6) Pallava—consists in applying the mantra at the end of the name of the medium: required in Māraṇa, or destructive rite.[1]

Many more technical matters of absorbing interest to those interested in Esoterism might be brought in and discussed here; but want of space prevents us from entering into the subject more in detail. Before closing this chapter, therefore, we will give a few references from the text of the *Sādhanamālā*, which provides more practical information on the subject. These observations are of special value, inasmuch as there are at present only a few scholars who are acquainted with the purely Tāntric doctrines and practices which were current among the Buddhists in the Tāntric age. The Buddhist Tantra insists that the mental condition of the worshipper in different rites should be different. In Śānti the mind should be peaceful. In Pauṣṭika it should have a thriving mentality. In Vaśīkaraṇa it should display anxiety, and in Māraṇa it should be in a greatly agitated state. Śānti should be performed on the first day of the lunar fortnight, Pauṣṭika on the full-moon day, Abhicāra or Māraṇa on the fourteenth day of the moon, and Vaśīkaraṇa on the eighth day. The worshipper should sit with his face northwards in Śānti, eastwards in Pauṣṭika, southwards in Abhicāra, and westwards in the rites of Ākarṣaṇa (attraction) and Uccāṭana. Śānti should be performed in autumn, Pauṣṭika in Hemanta, and Abhicāras in the summer season. Śānti should be performed in the evening, Pauṣṭika in the early morning, and Abhicāras at noon or at midnight.[2]

[1] See *Viśvakoṣa* (*Bengali*): article on षट्कर्म.

[2] See *Sādhanamālā*, pp. 368, 369.

It is not unnecessary to point out in this connexion that the deity worshipped in the different rites may be the same, but the same deity will have different colours, weapons and forms, in accordance with the rules guiding the rites, and it is precisely in this way that the deities of the Buddhist pantheon were multiplied.

CHAPTER X

LEADING TENETS

1. GURUS

IN ancient India, for all kinds of religious and secular knowledge, the necessity of a guru or a preceptor was always felt. The Upaniṣads were so called because the disciples had to sit near the guru to obtain knowledge of philosophical speculations directly from him. Also in secular literature, such as the *Arthaśāstra* of Kauṭilya and the *Kāmasūtra*, there are chapters on the Upaniṣads which contain such secret matters that lessons on these could be imparted to the disciple only through a direct channel by sitting near him. Similarly, the philosophical systems were handed down from gurus to disciples in an unbroken chain. In fact, the handing down of traditions through an uninterrupted chain of gurus and disciples is common with reference to all Śāstras that were produced in India; but nowhere is reverence to the guru so much in evidence as in Vajrayāna. Nothing, they affirm, can be achieved without a preceptor. It is impossible to follow mystic doctrines and practices without a preceptor. For what a particular mantra or a mystic practice is suited a person already initiated must be told by a preceptor, whose duty it is to inform him of the way in which it should be repeated, and the number of times it should be muttered, in order to attain the different kinds of perfections (Siddhis). The Buddhists always had preceptors, practically since the time of Buddha; but the more Buddhism became mystified in its later stages, the greater was the necessity for preceptors felt, and in Vajrayāna we find the position of the guru altogether paramount. He is idolized as the Buddha; he is the Sugata; he is Dharmakāya, and the bestowal of emancipation lies in his power. In every Tāntric work there is evidence of the high esteem in which the gurus were held,[1] and in many works the characteristics of the guru and the disciple are enumerated.[2] Simply because the mantra is known, and that correctly and accurately, there is no guarantee that by constantly muttering it one can attain perfection. It is well-nigh impossible, and it is against the principles of Vajrayāna. The worshipper is first to be initiated by the guru and he must obtain the different kinds of Abhiṣeka, or initiation, from the guru, and then, if all his instructions are followed in the most precise manner possible, then, and then alone, Siddhi is possible of attainment. Guru-ship is a position which is very difficult to attain; and, unless one answers to the characteristics laid down in the Vajrayāna literature, one is no guru but a cheat.[3]

2. Disciples

In view of the conflicting statements regarding the restrictions imposed on the worshippers of Vajrayāna, it becomes difficult to say how their lives were regulated in those times, and what mandates of the Church they had to follow. We find, for instance, that they must abstain from taking non-vegetarian food and abandon all kinds of objectionable foodstuff, such as onions, oil, salt, etc., and must not violate the rules of strict celibacy. In other places it is said that the offerings should consist of meat, wine and other objectionable articles. In the third place, again, it is said that the worship should be done after purifying the body by baths and by observing the rules of celibacy. In the fourth place, contrary to the above, no

[1] *Two Vajrayāna Works*, G.O.S., No. 44, p. 12, verses 9–16, where the guru is eulogized by the disciple.

[2] ibid., pp. 71 ff.

[3] ibid., p. 72.

अन्ये च गुरवः ख्याता मिथ्याज्ञानाभिमानिनः ।
लोभादर्थं प्रकुर्वन्ति धर्मस्य देशनां पराम् ॥

restriction is laid down either of place or of any particular food. Again, we also meet with a general rule that the worshipper obtains perfection by the muttering of mantras alone, even without drawing the magic circle or purifying himself by fasting.

The reason for this contradiction seems to be that the Vajrayānists recognized the existence of different grades among the worshippers and legislated for different classes, beginning with the strict observances of the Vinaya rules in the lowest rank to the stage of no restriction in the highest ranks. Indrabhūti recognized three classes of disciples, who had different degrees of mental development, and prescribed for them according to their mental capacities different regulations for their spiritual uplift.[1] Advayavajra classified the Buddhists as Śaikṣas and Aśaikṣas, and prescribed the strictest rules for the Śaikṣas who were less advanced. The Aśaikṣas, being much more advanced in the matter of spiritual progress, were allowed to follow such advanced practices as are prescribed in the higher forms of the Yogatantras.[2]

The Vajrayānists were thus divided into different classes by different authors; but the most popular classification is that in which the followers of Vajrayāna are divided into four classes. Kazi Dawasamdup divided Vajrayāna into six stages, though, of course, he regarded the different divisions as pertaining to Mantrayāna.[3] His divisions are:

(1) Kriyātantrayāna.
(2) Caryā- (or Upāya-) tantrayāna.
(3) Yogatantrayāna.
(4) Mahāyogatantrayāna.
(5) Anuttarayogatantrayāna.
(6) Atiyogatantrayāna.

[1] ibid., pp. 95 ff.

[2] *Advayavajrasaṁgraha*, op. cit., chap. I, p. 1.

[3] *Cakrasambhāratantra* (*Tāntric Texts*), intro., p. xxxii.

It is not, however, known on what authority this classification was based; and there is little hope of knowing it, as the reverend Kazi Saheb is now deceased. It is to be pointed out in this connexion that this elaborate system of classification was unknown in India, where only the Kriyātantra, Caryātantra, Yogatantra, Anuttarayogatantra[1] were known. These four terms are frequently met with in Buddhist Tāntric literature. Beginners and initiates into the mysteries of Vajrayāna were, of course, admitted to the lowest rank, namely the Kriyātantra, where strict rules of discipline and celibacy were enjoined on them until they were considered fit to be raised to a higher class. Yogatantra appears to have been reserved for those who were considered fit to come in contact with the Śaktis and to observe secret practices; while the Anuttarayogins belonged to the highest class and were immune from all laws, human or divine. The ascetics belonging to the last class were called the Siddhas, and were believed to be in possession of extraordinary powers of working diverse miracles and performing prodigious feats. The traditional number of Siddhas is recognized as eighty-four, and most of them belonged to the Pāla period of Bengal history.[2] The Tibetans are supposed to have preserved a history of the eighty-four Siddhas, and this has been translated into German by Arthur Grünwedel.

3. Bodhicitta

The Vajrayānist conception of the Bodhi mind appears to be the same as that of the Yogācāra school, which was founded by Maitreya and elaborated by Asaṅga, and the literature of which included, among others, such excellent works as the *Tattvasaṁgraha* of Śāntarakṣita. According to this school, the human mind, or, as it is called in Buddhism, the Bodhi mind, is something like a

[1] See Waddell, *Lamaism*, p. 152.

[2] Kern, *Manual of Buddhism*, p. 133.

continuous stream of momentary consciousness, which changes every moment the consciousness of the previous moment, giving rise to the consciousness of the succeeding moment, the former being the cause of the latter. This chain of momentary consciousness is without a beginning, or, at best, its starting-point cannot be traced; and Buddhism, more or less, is not so much concerned with the beginnings of things as it is with the future, or the emancipation of this chain of Vijñāna. This chain of momentary consciousness, operating in unison with the all-powerful act-force, leads itself either to degradation or to emancipation, depending on good or bad actions. The Bodhi mind is by nature surcharged with bad conformations—memory, desires, antipathies and false constructions (Kalpanā)—which consequently make it impure. To purify this chain of Vijñāna there should be an attempt on the part of its owner to remove the many impurities, and, until the impurities are fully removed, the Bodhi-mind will be subject to a series of transmigrations, not necessarily in the world of men, but in one of the numerous heavens, if the actions done are good; or in the world of animals, ghosts, etc., if the actions done are bad.[1]

As the impurities are removed, one after another, the Bodhi-mind commences an upward march in the different spiritual spheres, named by the Mahāyānists the Bhūmis, and stays in the different spheres only so long as he is not qualified to rise still higher or go down still lower. The number of these Bhūmis is generally recognized as ten, and the work which describes the ten Bhūmis and their characteristics, which qualify their occupants, is the famous *Daśabhūmikasūtra*, of which we have just got a magnificent edition from Dr. J. Rahder. The Bhūmis are named on page 5 of Dr. Rahder's book, and their names are: (1) Pramuditā, (2) Vimalā, (3) Prabhākarī, (4) Arciṣmatī, (5) Sudurajayā,

[1] B. Bhattacharyya, Foreword to the *Tattvasaṁgraha*, p. xxxix.

(6) Abhimukti, (7) Dūraṅgamā, (8) Acalā, (9) Sādhumatī, (10) and Dharmamedhyā.[1]

When the Bodhi-mind obtains emancipation, or, in other words, when it crosses all the ten Bhūmis mentioned above, it is rewarded with omniscience. Now, then, the question arises as to the place where the omniscient Bodhi-mind resides in the real cosmological structure, as conceived originally by Buddha.

In the Tāntric works generally the deities reside in the Akaniṣṭha heaven; but it appears, from the evidence obtained from the other sources, that they were inferior to the omniscient Bodhi-mind. The Bhūmis, it may be remembered, were not meant for the Hīnayānists; but were exclusively meant for the Mahāyānists, whose followers were called the Bodhisattvas. No Buddhist would be called a Bodhisattva, who has no compassion for suffering humanity or is not prepared to sacrifice his Nirvāṇa, even though entitled to it, until all creatures of the universe are in possession of the Bodhi knowledge. Thus, we can see how the Śrāvakas and Pratyekas are not entitled to the name of Bodhisattva, which also accounts for their being called Hīnayānists; because they selfishly look forward to their own benefit and are not at all moved by the intense sufferings of their other less-advanced brethren. The Hīnayānists, before obtaining their Nirvāṇa, have a place in the world structure; but their individuality is lost when they actually obtain Nirvāṇa. They have not to wait for the emancipation of others; and so the continuity of their existence is not at all necessary. But the Bodhi-mind of a Bodhisattva is entirely different. Even when the Bodhisattva is entitled to Nirvāṇa, he has to continue for the benefit of all living beings and work vigorously for their uplift. But the question arises as to what heavens they occupy, and where they go while obtaining omniscience. A satisfactory answer to this question

[1] op. cit., p. 5.

has been given by Śāntarakṣita, in his famous polemical work, the *Tattvasaṁgraha.*[1] There it is said:

अकनिष्ठपुरे रम्ये शुध्दावासविवर्जिते ।
बुध्यन्ते यत्र सम्बुध्दा निर्मितस्त्विह बुध्यते ॥

> In the excellent Akaniṣṭha heaven, which is beyond the Suddhāvāsa heaven, the Bodhisattva attains omniscience and (under his influence) a Buddha is born in this world.

Kamalaśīla, while commenting on this passage, adds the information that, beyond the Akaniṣṭha heaven, there is a Maheśvara Bhavana, or 'an abode of Maheśvara', where the chain of consciousness of the compassionate Bodhisattva attains omniscience. The Vajrayānist conception and definition of Bodhicitta is in accordance with the tenets of the Bodhisattvayāna, and it was first promulgated in the *Guhyasamāja.* According to this authority, the Bodhi-mind is that in which voidness and compassion work in unison.[2]

At this stage it is necessary to explain the conception of external objects from the viewpoint of Vajrayāna. In the eye of a Vajrayānist, the external world has much the same significance as it has in Yogācāra; and in the Tāntric works of the Buddhists there is ample evidence to show how the external world was treated in the philosophy of Vajrayāna. In one place it characterizes the external world, with its movable and immovable objects, such as a pot, picture, conveyance, house of statues, mountains, etc., as reduced by reason to mere appearances, in much the same way as magic and dreams are considered appearances. Therefore, the Vajrayānists held that external objects are no more real than

[1] p. 916.

[2] cf. *Two Vajrayāna Works*, p. 75, where the following line is quoted from the *Guhyasamāja*: शून्यताकरुणाभिन्नं बोधिचित्तमिति स्मृतम् ।

magic, a mirage, shadow or dream, and that their reality cannot be proved by reason.[1]

4. Ahaṁkāra

The peculiar feature of Vajrayāna worship lies in the doctrine of Ahaṁkāra, or the identification of the Bodhicitta with the deity worshipped. Ahaṁkāra is explained as 'I am the goddess and the goddess is in me'.[2] According to Ahaṁkāra, the worshipper should conceive himself as the deity, with the same complexion, form and limbs as described in the Sādhana, and should, instead of worshipping any external object, worship himself. It was suggested elsewhere that this rite of identification of the worshipper with the worshipped was a new feature, introduced for the first time by the Tāntric Buddhists. This has met with general criticism from a number of noteworthy scholars. They urged that, in view of the great antiquity of the Yoga philosophy, the contention that the doctrine of Ahaṁkāra is an introduction is untenable. To this it may be said, that the theory of the absorption of individual self with the Primordial Matter, or union of the self with a personal God, by the practice of Yoga, to attain thereby the perfect knowledge and the consequential freedom from the bondage of transmigration, was started in India from very ancient times, and traces of it can be found in the Upaniṣads of very great antiquity, even greater than than that of the Yoga system. Nothing, therefore, can be said to be an innovation; but still we say, for instance, that the Vedānta school originated with Śaṅkara, though previous to that there was a school of Aupaniṣada philosophers; that Śaṅkara systematized the doctrine of Māyā, though Buddhists from Nāgārjuna's time all acknowledged and wrote about the same

[1] For instance, *Sādhanamālā*, p. 139: चराचरं तत् सर्वं प्रतिभासमात्रं विचारेण प्रतिभासोपमं मायास्वप्नसदृशं, etc.

[2] For instance, ibid., p. 318: या भगवती प्रज्ञापारमिता साऽहं योऽहं सा भगवती प्रज्ञापारमिता ।

doctrine in their works. When, therefore, it is said that this element of Ahaṁkāra was introduced for the first time by Vajrayāna, it is said with reference to the identification of the worshipper with the deity, who is a transformation of the great reality known as Śūnya, not only for the purpose of attaining emancipation as is found in Yoga, but also for bewitching women, destroying men and their dwelling-houses, for the extraction of snake-poison, or for relieving a woman of the pains of labour. Ahaṁkāra, in fact, is imperative in the Vajrayāna form of worship, and this introduction is considered to be new in view of the multifarious purposes it is called upon to serve.

In some of the Hindu Tantras, indeed, this very doctrine of identification (or Ahaṁkāra) is to be found; and this fact gives rise to the controversy as to the priority, or otherwise, of the two predominant Tāntric schools, Hindu and Buddhist. There are sufficient reasons to hold that Hindu Tantras were introduced on the model of the Buddhist Tantras, and the Hindus, among others, borrowed many Buddhist customs, practices, deities and mantras. The very Kulācāra appears to have been already conceived by the Buddhists, and probably the forefathers of a large number of the Kaulas today were direct disciples of Buddhists in the Tāntric age. We are, therefore, not surprised to see Hindus making use of the Buddhist doctrine of Ahaṁkāra in their worship.

5. Advaya

To understand the significance of the Vajrayānist conception of Advaya, the theory of Śūnyatā and Karuṇā will have to be first taken into consideration. Voidness and compassion together constitute what is called Bodhicitta, or the Bodhi-mind. This idea, probably for the first time, makes its appearance in the *Guhyasamāja*. The mixing up of the two elements, Śūnyatā and Karuṇā, is what is known as Advaya.[1]

[1] cf. *Two Vajrayāna Works*, p. 75: शून्यताकरुणाभिन्नं . . . etc.

Śūnyatā, as conceived by the Vajrayānists, is very forcibly expressed in almost every Tāntric work of the Buddhists. Śūnyatā consists in thinking, or realizing, all worldly phenomena as transitory, momentary, non-ego, mistaken as realities by the mind, similar to objects seen in a dream or magic, endowed with inherent purity, non-existent, unborn and void, like the place of the Tathatā (thatness).[1]

The conception of compassion, or Karuṇā, of the Vajrayānists finds also a lucid expression in the Tāntric works. Compassion is defined there as the determination on the part of the Bodhisattva to lead to Nirvāṇa (and finally to place) all beings, including those born from eggs, the uterus, perspiration, those endowed with hoofs like horses, or whether with a form or formless, conscious or unconscious, or those who abide neither in consciousness nor in unconsciousness. In other places Karuṇā is defined as a strong determination to diffuse right knowledge among the people who, owing to desire (Tṛṣṇā), are blinded by ignorance, and cannot realize the continuous transmigration caused by the act-force; in order that they may lead a life in accordance with the law of dependent origination (Pratītya-samutpāda).[2]

The commingling of Śūnyatā with Karuṇā is designated by the Vajrayānists as Advaya, and it is a theory which is very important for understanding the underlying features of Vajrayāna, for on this alone the foundation of Śakti worship is based. Advaya is sometimes explained by means of a simile: 'As copper leaves its dirty colour and becomes gold when it comes in contact with the magic solution, even so the body leaves off its attachment, antipathies, etc., when it comes in contact with the tincture of Advaya.'[3] The commingling of Śūnyatā and Karuṇā is compared

[1] See *Sādhanamālā*, p. 111: अनित्याः क्षणिका निरात्मानः . . . etc.

[2] ibid., pp. 26, 111.

[3] ibid., p. 82: यथा सिध्दिरसेन विद्धं ताम्रं कृष्णतां त्यजति तथा शरीरमेवाद्वैतरसेन विद्धं रागद्वेषादिकं त्यजति ।

with salt melting in water, where the duality ceases, giving rise to non-duality, or Advaya. Just as other ideas were deified in Vajrayāna, Advaya was also deified, and we find two deities, Heruka and Prajñā, embodiments of Śūnya and Karuṇā, commingled in Advaya, and fused together in embrace in the Yuga-naddha, or the yab-yum form. The duality merges into one, and gives rise to the single form of Heruka only.

CHAPTER XI

PROCEDURE FOR WORSHIP

IT has been already pointed out that the Buddhists had a special literature which laid down the procedure for the worship of Tāntric deities of the Vajrayāna pantheon. The rules laid down in the Sādhanas are interesting as showing the way in which the old priests and the laity engaged themselves in medieval times, and as pointing out their particular beliefs and doctrines, and the way in which they utilized their knowledge and philosophy in actual practice. We will here take an elaborate Sādhana of Tārā, the Buddhist saviouress, which gives the procedure with a greater wealth of detail than most of the other Sādhanas.

First of all the worshipper is enjoined, after leaving the bed in the morning, to wash his face and feet, and repair to a place which is lonely and agreeable, and is anointed with scent and strewn with fragrant flowers. He should sit in an easy pose and meditate in his heart on the orb of the moon, which originates from the first vowel 'A', and notice thereunder a beautiful blue lotus in full bloom. On the filament of the lotus on which is placed the spotless moon, he should meditate on the germ syllable, 'Tāṁ', of yellow colour. Then from the yellow germ, 'Tāṁ', he should meditate on the rays of light issuing from it as destroying the darkness of ignorance of the world and as illumining the innumerable worlds that exist in the ten quarters, and as bringing from the firmament innumerable and inconceivable Buddhas and Bodhisattvas. Then, after an elaborate worship of these great compassionate Buddhas and Bodhisattvas by means of celestial flowers, incense, scents, garlands, unguents, powders, mendicant-dress, umbrellas, flags, bells, banners, and the like, he should make a confession of sins in the following manner: 'Whatever sinful deeds I have done, caused to be done, or allowed to be done, in this endless cycle of creation, everything I confess.' Again meditating on the restraint of wrong deeds, he should give his assent to meritorious deeds done by others with the words: 'I assent to the virtues of the Sugatas, Pratyekas, Śrāvakas, Jinas and their sons, the Bodhisattvas, and of the world with all the gods, beginning with Brahmā.' After this, refuge in the three jewels should be taken with the words: 'I take refuge in Buddha so long as the Bodhi essence subsists. I take refuge in Dharma so long as the Bodhi essence subsists; and I take refuge in Saṅgha so long as the Bodhi essence subsists.' Thereafter adherence to the path of the Tathāgata should be done with the words: 'By me should be followed only the path indicated by the Tathāgata, and naught else.' Then solicitation should be done with the words: 'The gods, the Tathāgatas and their children, who have created everything in this world for the benefit of the worldly beings, be constant to me and emancipate me.' Then a request should be made with the words: 'Gods and Tathāgatas, instruct me with such incontrovertible lessons on the law by which the beings of the world may be freed from the bond of the world quickly.' Then he should meditate on the results of his meritorious deeds with the following words: 'Whatever merit I have acquired by the seven kinds of extraordinary worship, such as the confession of sins, all that I devote to gain at the end the final Sambodhi.' Or otherwise he should recite the following, which indicates the seven kinds of extraordinary worship: 'All sins I confess and I gladly assent to the merits of others; for the sake of not having another birth, I take refuge in lord Buddha and in the Jewel of good Law, or in the three Jewels, and direct my thoughts to Bodhi. I follow his path and devote my merits to the attainment of Sambodhi.' With this the seven kinds of extraordinary worship should be performed, and then the gods, who have been invoked, should be dismissed with the mantra, Oṁ

Āḥ Muḥ, or with the following words: 'Thou movest now according to thy will, being anointed with the sandal of the Śīlas (commandments) and wearing the garments of Dhyāna (meditation) and being strewn with the flowers of the Bodhi limbs.'

Then the worshipper should meditate on the four Brahmas, namely friendship, compassion, happiness and indifference. What is meant by friendship? Its indication is the love that exists in all beings, such as the love towards an only son or like its fruition in their welfare and happiness. Compassion, again, is of what kind? It is the desire to save others from misery and from causes that lead to misery. The desire that I shall save even the people who are burnt with the great fire of suffering from the three evils and have entered the prison of Saṁsāra is what is known as Compassion; or it is the desire to save from the sea of Saṁsāra the beings suffering from the three evils. Happiness is of the following nature: It is that desire on the part of the worshipper to place all beings in this world in the sphere of Buddha-hood which they are unable to attain otherwise, or it is the attraction towards the virtues that exist in this world, and to their enjoyment and the spiritual powers arising out of them. What is indifference? Indifference consists in producing great welfare of all beings, good or bad, by discarding adverse requests and obstacles; or it is the desire that comes of its own accord to do good to all beings without the least expectation of reward; or it is the complete indifference to the eight human institutions of gain and loss, fame and notoriety, blame and praise, pleasure and pain, and all unusual activities. After meditating on the four Brahmas, the inherent purity of all worldly phenomena should be meditated. All worldly phenomena indeed are pure by nature, and, therefore, the worshipper should think himself pure by nature. This natural purity of all phenomena should be established by the mantra:

ॐ स्वभावशुद्धाः सर्वधर्माः स्वभावशुद्धोऽहम् ।

If all phenomena are naturally pure, where, then, is the possibility of the cycle of existence? Because of their being covered up with the impurity of such thought-categories as the subject and the object. This impurity can only be purged off by the meditation on the good path. By that it is restrained. Thus is established the essential and inherent purity of all phenomena.

After meditating on the purity of all phenomenal existence the voidness of all phenomena should be meditated upon. Here void means this. He should conceive the entire universe, with its mobile and immobile creations, as the clear manifestation of non-duality, when the mind is devoid of all kinds of false reflections and of such thought-categories as the subject and the object. This very voidness should be established by the mantra:

ॐ शून्यताज्ञानवज्रस्वभावात्मकोऽहम् ।

Then, as previously stated, in the heart the worshipper should meditate on the goddess, Āryatārā, who originates from the yellow germ syllable, 'Tāṁ', fixed on the orb of the spotless moon which is again on the filament of a full-blown blue lotus. The goddess, Tārā, should be conceived as sitting in Lalitāsana on the moon placed on the lotus, as one-faced and two-armed, showing the Varada Mudrā in the right hand and a blue lotus in the left, as profusely decorated with all kinds of ornaments, and of peaceful appearance. The goddess of this description should be conceived as long as desired. Then the eternally accomplished Bhagavatī should be drawn out by means of the rays that illumine the three worlds, the rays which issue forth from the yellow germ syllable, 'Tāṁ', placed on the orb of the moon, which is again within the filament of a beautiful blue lotus. After thus taking her out, she should be placed on the firmament and should be worshipped with the offerings of scented water and fragrant flowers, contained in the vessel inlaid with gems at the feet of the Bhagavatī. She should also be worshipped with various ceremonies, external and internal, by means of flowers, incense, light-stick, food-offerings, scents, garlands, unguents, powders, mendicant-dress, umbrella, flags, bell, banner, and the like. Thus after repeatedly worshipping and praising her, the Mudrā, or the mystic pose of the hand, should be exhibited. After propitiating the goddess of the essence of knowledge with this Mudrā, she should be commingled with the goddess of the essence of Samaya, and by so doing the non-duality of the two should be established and meditated upon. Then the rays that issue from the yellow germ syllable, 'Tāṁ', which is on the spotless moon, illuminate the worlds in the ten quarters, cause the removal of poverty and other miseries of the beings that inhabit them by showers of various gems; and they (rays) impart to them the teachings on the realization of the momentary Śūnya. After doing beneficial deeds for the worldly beings, the worshipper should meditate on the form of Tārā which is identified with the universe. Again he should meditate repeatedly until tired the yellow germ syllable and the Bhagavatī contained therein. He who is unable to meditate in this fashion should mutter the mantra, Oṁ Tāre Tuttāre Ture Svāhā. This is the lord of all mantras. It is endowed with great powers, and is saluted, worshipped and revered by all the Tathāgatas. After finishing the Dhyāna, he should think of the world as the form of Tārā, and should move about considering himself to be the Bhagavatī. Generally all the eight great Siddhis fall at the feet of those who meditate on the Bhagavatī in this manner, not to speak of other smaller perfections which come as a matter of course. Whoever meditates on the Bhagavatī in a lonely mountain cave espies her with his own eyes; the Bhagavatī herself gives him his very breath, nay, more, even the Buddha-hood, which is most difficult to attain, remains as if it is in the palm of his hand.[1]

[1] This represents a free translation of the Kiñcitvistara-Tārā Sādhana, composed by Anupama Rakṣita, the Sthavira: *Sādhanamālā*, Sādhana No. 98.

CHAPTER XII

THE DEITIES

IT is due to the Tāntric Buddhists that Buddhism can boast of an extensive and varied pantheon of gods, whose aids were invoked for all kinds of perfections and Siddhis described before. The deities were of various colours and of various forms, and were invoked to discharge multifarious functions. These deities were represented either in stone or in metal and paintings, in order to provide an aid to the worshipper for conceiving their forms and identifying himself with the deities in question. Vajrayāna had made itself attractive and popular by its interesting tenets, doctrines and practices, and the exquisite art they had developed in representing images, especially in stone and metal, proved doubly attractive, and helped the priests in converting a large number of people and bringing them into their fold. The conception of the deities is inseparably connected with the Vajrayāna philosophy, and is especially so with the conception of Śūnya. According to the Buddhist Tantras, the deities of the pantheon are all manifestations of Śūnya.[1] Advayavajra, who was a contemporary of the Pāla king, Mahīpāla I, who flourished between A.D. 978 and 1030, in a characteristic stanza says that the deities are nothing but manifestations of Śūnya and are by nature non-existent; and whenever there is manifestation it must be Śūnya in essence.[2] In another place the process of evolution of deities from Śūnya is explained in an interesting stanza by the

[1] B. Bhattacharyya, *Indian Buddhist Iconography*, p. 166.

[2] *Advayavajrasaṁgraha*, p. 51:

स्फूर्तिश्च देवताकारा निःस्वभावाः स्वभावतः ।
यथा यथा भवेद् स्फूर्तिः सा तथा शून्यतात्मिका ॥

same author. The process of evolution has four stages: the first is the right perception of Śūnyatā, or voidness; the second is the connexion with the germ syllable, the Bīja; the third is the conception of an Icon; and the fourth is the external representation of the deities.[1] This statement gives a direct lie to the theory that later Buddhism was nothing but gross idolatry. It shows, on the other hand, that their conception of godhead was philosophically most profound, a parallel to which is scarcely to be found in any other Indian religion.

Occasionally information is obtained about the residence of the deities contained in the pantheon; and, so far as can be gathered from the stray references, it can be asserted without hesitation that the abode of the Vajrayāna deities was in the Akaniṣṭha heaven, which is the topmost of the Rūpa heavens.[2] It has been pointed out before that the deities of the Vajrayāna system represent Śūnya, and they are Śūnya in essence with the three elements, Śūnya, Vijñāna and Mahāsukha. They are rather the voluntary manifestions of Śūnya, in accordance with the Bīja mantra uttered by the worshipper, with an appearance suitable for the function the deity has to discharge. Sometimes deities are described as equal to all Tathāgatas, and by Tathāgatas they mean the five Dhyāni Buddhas. The implication of this is that the deities are an embodiment of the five Skandhas, over each of which one Dhyāni Buddha presides[3]—such as Akṣobhya for Vijñāna; Vairocana for Rūpa; Ratnasambhava for Vedanā; Amitābha for Saṁjñā, and Amoghasiddhi for Saṁskāra. When one element among the five predominates, the deity is considered to be the emanation of that Dhyāni Buddha who presides over the element in question. When such a deity is represented in art, he bears

[1] ibid., p. 50 शून्यताबोधितो बीजं बीजाद्बिम्बं प्रजायते । बिम्बे च न्यासविन्यासौ, etc.

[2] See *Sādhanamālā*, pp. 47, 64, etc.

[3] cf. *Two Vajrayāna Works*, p. 41:

पंचबुद्धस्वभावत्वात् पंचस्कन्धा जिनाः स्मृताः ।

on his head the same Dhyāni Buddha, and is considered his offspring and as belonging to his family. The other Dhyāni Buddhas are generally represented on the aureole over the head of the principal deity.

The Buddhist Tantras are particular to have a colour applied to all deities. This colour has a deep spiritual significance, and is a thing which should not be passed over unnoticed. The Dhyāni Buddhas have each a different colour, and the deities emanating from each of the Dhyāni Buddhas, constituting his family, should ordinarily have the same colour as that of their spiritual father. Thus the family of Akṣobhya—the embodiment of the Vijñāna-skandha—should have a blue colour, because it is the colour of the Dhyāni Buddha Akṣobhya. This is, of course, the general rule; but numerous exceptions are also found. Let us take, for instance, a deity who is very popular and has the power to grant success in a variety of protective and destructive rites. The deity cannot have the same colour in all the rites, because the difference in rites demands a difference in form, colour, posture, and so forth.[1] This is why occasionally we find difference of colour amongst the members belonging to the same family.

It is frequently seen from the texts that the deities sometimes present a fierce appearance and are invoked in terrible rites, such as the destruction of men (Māraṇa) and their houses (Uccāṭana), and so forth. Perhaps the authors considered this incompatible with the theory of compassion, and a few indirect explanations to clear up the point became necessary. Two characteristic passages are quoted below; one with reference to the fierce form of Yamāri and the other in respect of Ucchuṣma Jambhala.

श्रीमन्तमन्तःकरुणामयं तं
सत्त्वार्थहेतोर्बहिरुग्ररूपम् ।

[1] cf., for instance, p. 556, कर्मानुरूपतो वर्णे ; p. 395, कर्मानुरूपतः शुक्लादिवर्णयुक्तां ; p. 532, रक्तकृष्णसितवर्णे कर्मानुरूपतो ध्येयम् ।

नाथं यमारिं प्रणिपत्य मूर्ध्ना
लिखामि तत्साधनमिष्टहेतोः ॥[1]

After making my obeisance by my head to Lord Yamāri, who is of dignified appearance; internally compassionate, but externally terrific for the good of all beings, I write the procedure of his worship for the benefit of all.

दारिद्र्यदुःखाहतमानसानां
का चित्तवृत्तिः सुगतस्य कृत्ये ।
अतश्च कोपादिव जम्भलोऽसौ
उच्छुष्मरूपं भयदं चकार ॥[2]

People who are stricken down with the misery of poverty, what desire can they have for the rites laid down by Sugata? It is for this reason, it seems, that Jambhala in his anger assumed the terrific form of Ucchuṣma.

According to the Tāntrics, therefore, though the deities appear terrific externally, they are nevertheless extremely compassionate internally; and they always engage themselves in doing good to the worshipper. It becomes sometimes necessary for the deities to assume a terrible form in order to overawe and coerce people to perform the rites laid down by Sugata.

Mahākāla is another very terrible deity, with terrible appearance, who is invoked to discharge terrible functions. Neither his appearance nor his functions are in keeping with the doctrine of Karunā, or compassion, taught in the Vajrayāna Buddhism. But the shrewd priests offer for this an excellent explanation. They say:

आचार्ये यः सदा द्वेषी कुपितो रत्नत्रयेऽपि यः ।
अनेकसत्त्वविध्वंसी महाकालेन खाद्यते ॥[3]

One who is persistently a hater of the preceptor and is adversely disposed towards the three jewels—Buddha,

[1] *Sādhanamālā*, p. 550. [2] ibid., 570. [3] ibid., p. 586.

Dharma and Saṅgha—and immolates many animals, is eaten up alive by Mahākāla.

Now, in a case like this, we can easily understand that the conception of the fierce form of Mahākāla is quite in keeping with the doctrine of compassion, because such a person is incorrigible, and he, alone and unaccompanied, does harm to many beings, and a mischievous person like him ought to be removed by the fierce deity called Mahākāla for the good of many. We cannot, however, perceive the necessity of eating the poor offender alive, unless, of course, it is assumed that his mental condition will change materially, at least in the next birth, by undergoing a transformation in the compassionate stomach of Mahākāla!

Occasionally a charge is laid at the door of later Buddhism that it is a form of gross idolatry. Those who hold this theory are not quite correct in this estimation, and it is necessary to show in detail that Buddhist worship had nothing to do with idolatry. Idolatry means worship of idols. It has many drawbacks; but it is very useful for society as a whole. The formless abstraction and unseen power, which we characterize as God, is a thing very difficult to be conceived even by great ascetics, not to speak of the common people, who have no idea of what attributes God actually represents. If, of course, as we generally do through the medium of images, we can make the mass believe in the great unseen power and His unbounded compassion for suffering humanity, and make them fear sin and love piety, then we must necessarily admit that idol worship is fraught with great utility and is of great social service. But that is no reason for considering idol worship logical, unless we can definitely prove the actual possession of the image by God, when a few apparently meaningless words are uttered for the infusion of the image with life. This is indeed very difficult to believe in this scientific age, and it is one of the reasons why image worship has been characterized by some as grossly superstitious, and image worshippers as idolators. Idol worship has its utility in its own sphere; and in India it has been considered a necessity from very ancient times. But on the ground of public utility, as such, it can have no scientific value; because we have never authoritatively known that a deity ever actually takes possession of the image prepared for the purpose. The Hindus worship idols in this way and believe that their mantras can infuse their image with life; and therefore they are, to all intents and purposes, idolators.

The Jainas regard their images as remembrancers; by seeing the images of their Tīrthaṅkaras, whom they believe to be historical personages, they call to mind their noble lives, excellent deeds, their lofty preachings, their high ideals, and to their memory they offer various articles of worship in token of reverence. Their idol worship is not exactly what can be called idolatry in so far as these Tīrthaṅkaras are concerned. But the moment they leave this sphere and offer objects of worship to hypothetical beings, such as the Yakṣas and the Yakṣiṇīs, with four faces and eight arms, or with other abnormalities and with strange vehicles, they are relegated to the sphere of idolatry. For here, also, we cannot prove that these strange creatures ever existed on the face of the earth.

But the Buddhist mode of worship is entirely different from that of the Hindus or of the Jainas. To the Buddhist, the external world has no existence. Even the body with its sense organs is unreal. The real noumenon is only Śūnya, which, together with Karuṇā, constitutes the Bodhicitta. The Bodhi-mind, then, is also a reality; in fact, it has the same reality as that of Śūnya, and beyond the mind there is nothing in the external world. The body, as such, being external, does not exist: and it has no reality. This is the conception of the mind and of the external world in Vajrayāna. To the followers of Vajrayāna, therefore, how can there be reality in an image, a grossly external object to which worship may be offered? The Vajrayāna theory of godhead is so peculiar, and had such successive stages of development, traceable through the Buddhist literature for several centuries, that whenever similar conceptions or theories are met with in literature or in religion of other sects, we can easily put our finger on them and characterize them as borrowed from the later Buddhism.

The worshipper is generally designated as the Bodhisattva. After following the prescribed procedure, according to the instructions of the guru or according to the instructions laid down in the Tāntric works, he should regard himself as nothing but a chain of momentary consciousness, full of compassion for suffering humanity, and invoke the aid of Śūnya with the three elements: Śūnya, Vijñāna and Mahāsukha. This aid can be invoked only when the Bodhi-mind of the Bodhisattva is completely identified with Śūnya, and only when this is done the Śūnya responds. In accordance with the Bīja mantra, or in accordance with the purpose for which the aid of Śūnya is invoked, it transforms itself into the form of a divinity with which the Bodhi-mind is identified. When the commingling of the Bodhi-mind with the deity takes place, the former develops great power and is able to do the work for which the deity has been invoked, until the latter is dismissed from the mind by the proper formula. A glance at the list of deities and the aims and objects of Vajrayānists will show the multifarious duties Śūnya had to perform, and into how many forms it had to transform itself. It can, indeed, be pointed out that because of the large number of images of gods and goddesses of the Vajrayāna pantheon made and subsequently discovered from under the earth; therefore the Buddhists must be considered idolators. Against this it can be pointed out that it is not always an easy task to conceive the outward appearance of gods and goddesses of an extensive pantheon for the purpose of meditation without the help of images or pictures, and it is in order to supply this most important aid to numerous worshippers that innumerable images had to be made of stone, metal or earth. We have evidence also that pictures were painted for the same purpose, and even now in Nepal the Vajrācāryas keep a large stock of paintings and pictures of an overwhelming number of gods and goddesses for their numerous clients. It must be definitely understood that an attempt is made here to represent the case of the Buddhists with regard to the charge of idolatry occasionally levelled at them. From a study of their literature, we can definitely proclaim that Vajrayāna was no idolatry. But if some ignorant lay disciple, in imitation of the Hindu and Jaina customs, offers a few flowers at the foot of the image, it need not impugn the pure doctrine of the Śāstras.

The attitude of the Buddhist priests towards Hindu religion and its gods and goddesses was entirely unfavourable, if not antagonistic.[1] They were not only hostile to the Hindu gods; but their hostility proves further that they had a great hatred towards the members of other religions also. In the Buddhist Tantras we find a number of Hindu gods insulted, calumniated and humiliated. A number of Buddhist gods are seen displaying the Brahmaśiras, or the head of Brahmā, with four faces and grey beards. As Brahmā is the first member of the Hindu trinity, this signifies the hatred the Buddhist priests had for Hindu gods in particular and Hinduism in general. Harihariharivāhanodbhava, a form of Avalokiteśvara, the all-compassionate Bodhisattva, has for his Vāhana (or favourite animal), Viṣṇu, the second god of the Hindu trinity. The latter cannot be mistaken for any other god, because in the description his own favourite Vāhana, the mythical bird, Garuḍa, is present. In the description of Caṇḍaroṣaṇa, the god carries the noose in order to bind the enemies who cause suffering to humanity, such as Viṣṇu, Śiva, and Brahmā, who are terrified by the raised index finger of the god. Further on, it is

[1] But Dr. Coomaraswami, of Boston, has no faith in this, and, in fact, in the mass of evidence collected here. J.A.O.S., Vol. 46, p. 187.

directed that Caṇḍaroṣaṇa should be conceived as locking towards the miserable people who are subjected to constant revolution in the cycle of existence by the wicked gods, Viṣṇu, Brahmā, Śiva and Kandarpa, the god of love. By Caṇḍaroṣaṇa's intervention, the hosts of terrified and weeping Māras, who are nude, with dishevelled hair and hopeless in despair, are hacked to pieces by the sword carried by the deity. Caṇḍaroṣaṇa gives their life back and places them near his feet, so that they may perform pious deeds in future. While enumerating the benefits that accrue from the worship of the Mṛtyuvañcana Tārā, it is said that the worshipper conquers death and gets emancipated, and even the ends of his hair cannot be destroyed by the Hindu gods, such as Brahmā, Indra, the Moon, the Sun, Śiva, the deities of the waters, Yama and Manmatha. Again, while describing Mārīcī, the principal Hindu gods are brought to the humiliating position of making obeisance to Mārīcī. Some of them are actually trampled under her feet, while others obey her orders like servants. In another place it is said that to the ascetic who pleases the goddess Kurukullā, come Brahmā, Rudra, Indra, Nārāyaṇa, and others, and meet all his wants like servants. While describing Vajrajvālānalārka, he is characterized as trampling under his foot not only Viṣṇu, but also his consort, Lakṣmī. Bhūtaḍāmara is described as an expert in destroying the pride of Indra, Brahmā, Kubera, and others. Ucchuṣma Jambhala is described as pressing Kubera under his feet, so that he may vomit jewels. Trailokya-vijaya tramples upon the head of Śiva and the bosom of Gaurī, who lie on the ground in opposite directions. Prasannatārā is described as trampling upon Indra and Upendra, and pressing Rudra and Brahmā between his legs. Paramāśva is described as four-legged, and as trampling with the first right leg on Indrāṇī and Lakṣmī, with the second right Rati and Prīti, with the first left Indra and Madhukara, and with the second left Jayakara and Vasanta. While describing the merits and advantages to be gained by worshipping Hayagrīva, an exceedingly attractive prospect of future happiness is held before the public, but not without calumniating a number of Hindu gods. The worshipper, when he attains perfection, goes to the Vidyādhara land, installs himself as king, and enjoys all sorts of pleasures. All Hindu gods flock together to him, and he assigns various duties to the different gods. Aparājitā is described as a goddess, whose parasol is raised over her head by wicked and mischievous gods, such as Brahmā and others.[1]

Now the above are a few among many instances where Hindu gods are insulted and made subservient to Buddhist gods; but these are instances found in writing. The same happened in practice. A large number of images was carved by the followers of Vajrayāna, which represented in stone the Hindu gods being humiliated by Buddhist gods, and the same occurs in painting. Ganeśa is regarded by the Hindus as the bestower of perfection and success in Tāntric rites. The Buddhists, in order to display their aversion towards the Brāhmaṇical faith, made their gods trample upon Gaṇeśa. Thus in the Indian Museum images of Parṇaśavarī and Aparājitā, the Calcutta Vaṅgīya Sāhitya Pariṣad image of Vighnāntaka, the deities have been represented as trampling Gaṇeśa under their feet. In the two Vikramapur images of Parṇaśavarī and the Dacca Sāhitya Pariṣad image of Mahāpratisarā, Gaṇeśa appears below the lotus seat, lying prostrate on the ground under the pressure of Buddhist deities. The Buddhists showed their animosity towards the Hindu god, Gaṇeśa, and gave him the epithet of Vighna, or obstacle. In the Bodhgaya image of Trilokyavijaya, the deity is represented as trampling upon the prostrate forms of Śiva and Gaurī. In the Nepal images of Harihariharivāhana,

[1] *Sādhanamālā*, intro., p. cxxxi f., footnotes, where these references have been collected. See also pp. 77, 174, 175, 214, 241, 300, 350, 403, 510, 511, 512, 571.

Avalokiteśvara rides on the shoulders of Viṣṇu, exactly in the same way as Viṣṇu rides Garuḍa. In the Vikramapur images of Parṇaśavarī, Hayagrīva, the Hindu god of fever, and Śītalā, the Hindu goddess of smallpox, are seen running away in opposite directions from the mere presence of the more powerful Buddhist goddess. This is how the Buddhists of the Tāntric age attempted to exhibit the superiority of their gods over those of the Brāhmaṇical faith.[1]

The Tāntric Buddhists did not spare the pet but unscientific theories of the Hindus regarding salvation. For instance, they attacked the doctrine of holy Tīrthas in unequivocal language. In this connexion, a passage quoted from the *Cittaśodhanaprakaraṇa* of Āryadeva, a later Tāntric writer, is interesting. He says:

प्रतरन्नपि गंगायां नैव श्वा शुध्दिमर्हति ।
तस्माध्दर्मधियां पुंसां तीर्थस्नानं तु निष्फलम् ॥
धर्मो यदि भवेत् स्नानात् कैवर्तानां कृतार्थता ।
नक्तन्दिवं प्रविष्टानां मत्स्यादीनां तु का कथा ॥
पापक्षयोऽपि स्नानेन नैव स्यादिति निश्चयः ।
यतो रागादिबुध्दिस्तु दृश्यते तीर्थसेविनाम् ॥[2]

> A dog swimming in the Ganges is not considered pure; therefore, bathing in holy places is futile for pious men. If bathing can confer merit, the fishermen must be most meritorious; not to speak of fish and other aquatic animals, who are always in water, day and night. It is certain that by bathing even sin is not dissipated, because people who are in the habit of making pilgrimages are full of passion, hatred and other vices.

[1] B. Bhattacharyya, *Indian Buddhist Iconography*, p. 162.

[2] From *Cittaśodhanaprakaraṇa* of Āryadeva, published by Mm. Haraprasād Śāstrī, in J.A.S.B., 1898, pp. 117 ff.

CHAPTER XIII

THE PANTHEON

THE varied, extensive and diversified pantheon ot the Northern Buddhists owes its origin to Tāntric Buddhism, or Vajrayāna. There are certain indications that Buddhism had no pantheon before Tāntrism was well established. In earlier Buddhism it recognized thirty-three gods of the Hindus, who were residents of the Trāyastriṁśa heaven, which is one among the many Rūpa heavens. Buddha did not believe in gods, and in *Saundarananda* we find Buddha discouraging Nanda from touching his feet in token of worship. He told him he would not be in the least pleased by Nanda's taking the dust of his feet, but he would bless him if he would follow the precepts laid down in Buddhism and practise true Saddharma. Buddha was deified in Mahāyāna, which considered him to be Lokottara, or superhuman.[1] In Buddhist art also we do not find any of his images in any of the earlier schools, such as the Sāñchi and Bharhut schools, and it is believed that the Græco-Buddhists of Gāndhārā were the first to carve out his image from stone.[2] Without going into a discussion as to the correctness or otherwise of this theory, we can only remark, while passing, that in the Gāndhāra school alone we meet with a profuse number of images of Buddha. A number of gods and goddesses are described in the *Mañjuśrīmūlakalpa*, which is believed to have been written in about the second century A.D.; also in the *Prajñāpāramitā* we find a description of elaborate worship of Buddha with diverse paraphernalia. But even then,

[1] cf. *Mahāvastu*, Vol. I, p. 2: आर्यमहासाङ्घिकानां लोकोत्तरवादिनां मध्यदेशिकानां, etc.

[2] Theory first advanced by Prof. A. Foucher in *Beginnings of Buddhist Art and Other Essays*, p. 127. Dr. Coomaraswami thinks that the Mathurā school can also have a claim to the production of the earliest image of Buddha.

it does not seem clear that the Buddhists had any conception of a well-defined and well-classified pantheon. It is in the *Guhyasamāja* that we find the idea of a Buddhist pantheon properly crystallized; here, for the first time, we find the description of the five Dhyāni Buddhas, their mantras, their Maṇḍalas and their Śaktis. These Dhyāni Buddhas represented the five Skandhas, or elements, of which the world is composed. They are here described as the progenitors of five Kulas, or families. Here we read:

द्वेषमोहस्तथा रागश्चिन्तामणिसमयस्तथा ।
कुला ह्येते तु वै पञ्च काममोक्षप्रसाधकाः ॥ [1]

> The five Kulas are Dveṣa, Moha, Rāga, Cintāmaṇi and Samaya, which conduce to the attainment of all desires and emancipation.

The emanations, or offspring, of these Dhyāni Buddhas constitute their families. It was in this way that the Buddhists got a systematized and well-classified pantheon, with its profusion of gods and goddesses. When these were represented in art they were required to show their origin by holding on their head the miniature figure of their parental Dhyāni Buddha. Each deity was given various forms, with two hands, four hands, six hands, eight hands, or even up to twenty-four, and proportionately one to four heads, and up to twelve heads. They were given different colours, different companions and different expressions, in accordance with their worship in the different Tāntric rites, and in accordance with the different functions they were required to discharge, from curing a disease to killing an enemy. The artist had a considerable hand in designing the images of deities, and they introduced their own traditions and innovations. The votaries also, according as they wanted to have their gods in more or less powerful forms, added extra hands, heads and feet, to suit

[1] *Guhyasamāja*, op. cit., pp. 6, 11, 16–17.

their own ideas and whims; and it was precisely in this way that the deities increased to an amazing number.

It has already been indicated that the *Guhyasamāja* went into private hands after its inception, and was handed down through an unbroken chain of gurus and disciples for three hundred years; and obtained publicity, through the teachings and mystic songs of the Buddhist Siddhācāryas and Vajrācāryas, in about the middle of the seventh century. It is for this reason that we do not find references to this pantheon in the general Buddhist literature, or in the works of the Chinese travellers who came to India to investigate the condition of Buddhism prevalent in their own time. Despite this fact, certain names of Buddhist gods and goddesses are indeed found in these writings, though they do not pertain to the well-classified pantheon referred to above. In the *Sukhāvatī-vyūha*,[1] which was translated into Chinese between A.D. 148 and 170, the name of Amitābha appears for the first time, who was the presiding deity of the Sukhāvatī or the Akaniṣṭha heaven, where he is believed to have brought Avalokiteśvara into existence. We should remember that in the Vajrayāna works also this heaven has been characterized as the abode of all deities. In the smaller recension of the same work, which was also translated into Chinese between A.D. 384 and 417, mention is made of two more gods, namely Akṣobhya as a Tathāgata and Mañjuśrī as a Bodhisattva. Fa-hien (A.D. 394 to 414) mentions the names of Mañjuśrī, Avalokiteśvara and the future Buddha Maitreya; and Hiuen-thsang (A.D. 629 to 645) the names of Avalokiteśvara, Hārīti, Kṣitigarbha, Maitreya, Mañjuśrī, Padmapāṇi, Vaiśravaṇa, Śākyabuddha, Śākya-Bodhisattva and Yama, as also the names of deified saints such as Aśvaghoṣa, Nāgārjuna, Asaṅga, Sumedhas, and others. I-Tsing (A.D. 671 to 695) mentions the names of Avalokiteśvara, Amitāyus or Amitābha, Hārīti, the Caturmahārājikas, Maitreya, Mañjuśrī,

[1] Ed. Max Müller, in *Anecdota Oxoniensia*, pp. 1, 28, 32.

Yama, besides several others. Śāntideva (A.D. 695 to 730), in his *Sikṣāsamuccaya*, mentions the names of Akṣobhya as a Tathāgata, Gaganagañja as a Bodhisattva, Siṁhavikrīḍita as a Tathāgata, Cundā, Trisamayarāja, Mārīcī, Siṁhanāda, Mañjughoṣa, and many others. After Śāntideva the Tantras of the Buddhists got wide publicity; and in the Tāntric works written after his time all referred to the pantheon, and described many gods who were included in it. The Sādhana literature, which describes the forms of gods and the procedure for worshipping them, was developed by the Siddhācāryas Saraha, Nāgārjuna, Śabarīpā, Anaṅgavajra, Indrabhūti, and many others, though the earliest Sādhana was perhaps written by Asaṅga, who flourished in the third century A.D., in which he referred to the Dhyāni Buddhas and their emanations.[1]

When we examine the images executed in the different schools of art, we also come to the same conclusion, that the Buddhist pantheon was not well-developed before the Tantras got wide publicity, in about the beginning of the eighth century. In the Gāndhāra school, for instance, besides the Buddha images we meet with the images of Jambhala, Maitreya, Hārīti (the Indian Madonna) and her consort, along with other Bodhisattva images.[2] In the Mathurā school of sculpture, which was either contemporaneous or somewhat later than the Gāndhāra school, we meet with numerous Buddha and Bodhisattva images, and those of Kubera, Yakṣas and Nāgas. The Mathurā school extended to the early Gupta period, and here also we do not meet with the later Buddhist gods, namely Avalokiteśvara, Mañjuśrī, Tārā, and the like.[3] The case of the Magadha school, which flourished after the Mathurā school, is otherwise. It included the images of Sāranāth, Nālandā

[1] Sādhana No. 159, in the *Sādhanamālā*.

[2] V. A. Smith, *Fine Art in India and Ceylon*, Figs. 62, 63, Pl. XXVIII, Figs. 64, 65; also Garuḍa and Nāga images, Fig. 70; refer also to the image of Kubera, No. 3912 of the Indian Museum.

[3] *A.S.I. Ann. Rep.*, 1906–7, p. 145; *Mathura Museum Catalogue*, pp. 27–28.

and Odantapuri. The most flourishing period of the Magadha school was contemporaneous with the reign of the Pāla kings of Bengal, and lasted till the Muhammadan conquest of Eastern India.[1] In this school we find the first reference to a well-classified pantheon; because in most of the images there are five Dhyāni Buddhas round the aureole over the head, as also the miniature of the parental Dhyāni Buddha on their crowns. Again, unlike the Gāndhāra and Mathurā schools, there is a great dearth of Buddha images, and, even when he is represented, he takes the form of Vajrāsana, being flanked by Avalokiteśvara and Maitreya on the two sides in a semi-mythical form. In the Magadha school, therefore, Buddha partakes of the nature of the Dhyāni Buddha Akṣobhya, as is evident from the numerous Sādhanas dedicated to his worship. The Bodhisattva images also are not so stereotyped as we find them in Gāndhāra and Mathurā. The Magadha school is characterized by its wide variety of images of gods and goddesses; and this will be apparent to any visitor who goes to the museums at Sāranāth and Nālandā, or Patna, or takes a turn in the extensive ruins of the Odantapuri Vihāra, now situated near the railway station at Bihar, on the Bihar Bakhtiyarpur Light Railway. At Sāranāth we meet with the images of Ṣaḍakṣarī Lokeśvara, Ucchuṣma Jambhala, Mañjuśrī, Tārā, Vasudhārā, Mārīcī, all the five Dhyāni Buddhas, Vajrasattva, the sixth Dhyāni Buddha, and many others belonging to the Vajrayāna pantheon. Almost the same variety of images presents itself in Nālandā and Sāranāth.

The Bengal school of art, which comes next, was distinguished by the high-class art it produced and for its beauty in execution. Its flourishing period ranged from the tenth century, or earlier, to the conquest of Bengal by the Muhammadans. Many of the specimens of the Bengal school are preserved in the museums at Calcutta, Dacca, Rajshahi and the Vaṅgīya Sāhitya Pariṣad, and a

[1] V. A. Smith, *History of Fine Art in India and Ceylon*, p. 146.

PLATE II

VAJRĀSANA

large number of them are scattered about in the Pargana Vikrampur, in the districts of Dinajpur and Comilla. In this school many interesting images of gods belonging to the Tāntric Buddhism are to be met with; and from these it seems clear that the artists were acquainted with a large number of descriptions of the form of gods as given in the Sādhana literature; for instance, among others there are images of Heruka, Vasudhārā, Jambhala, Arapacana, Khasarpaṇa, Parṇaśavarī, Siṁhanāda, Mañjuvara, Aparājitā, Mahāpratisarā, Nairātmā, Ṣaḍakṣarī Lokeśvara, Mahāśrī Tārā, Khadiravaṇī Tārā, and many others.[1]

The images of Buddhist deities found at Ajanta, Ellora and in South India show signs of an immature development of Tantra, and may be assigned to a period prior to the Bengal school, though the paintings of Ajanta and other sculptures are of great antiquity. Javanese art was profoundly influenced by the Bengal school of art, and the images of gods and goddesses as found in the Bodo-budur temple show that they knew many deities of the Vajrayāna pantheon.[2] As Vajrayāna was mainly a product of Bengal, it is probable that the Bengal colonists carried their art and religion to Java by the sea route, probably from Tāmralipti, which is even now regarded as a seaport.

After the destruction of Buddhism in India, the priests of the celebrated monasteries of Bengal and Magadha, who could save their heads from the hostile swords of Muhammadanism, fled to Nepal, which is protected on all sides by the natural ramparts of the Himalayas, and took refuge in that country, and thus kept the torch of Buddhism still burning there. The Bengal school of

[1] Most of these images are reproduced in *Indian Buddhist Iconography*, in their appropriate places. The latest contribution on the subject of the Bengal school of art, with numerous illustrations of Hindu and Buddhist images, is represented by N. K. Bhaṭṭaśālī, *Iconography of Buddhist and Brahmanical Sculptures in the Dacca Museum, 1929.*

[2] Dr. J. Ph. Vogel, *The Relation Between the Art of India and Java*, p. 14.

art was carried there; but it was soon modified when it came in contact with the native artists, and was thus stereotyped. The general impression of the visitor who visits the numerous monasteries in Nepal, which are a repository of a large number of images of the diverse Buddhist deities, is that the excellences of the Bengal school could not be preserved by the Nepal artists, and that decadence in art was already in evidence. The followers of Vajrayāna, who went to Nepal in order to make sure of their existence, converted a good many Newars of the land to Buddhism, and carved innumerable images of gods and goddesses in stone, metal and wood, so much so that a student of iconography is overwhelmed by their wealth and variety.

The cumulative evidence of art, history, philosophy and literature leads us to believe that the pantheon of the Northern Buddhists was not widely known before the eighth century A.D., nor was the underlying philosophy, which may warrant the formation of a pantheon, well-developed before that time, though the origin of the latter may have been considerably earlier. This may be explained by the fact that the *Guhyasamāja*, which for the first time inculcated the doctrine of the five Dhyāni Buddhas and their families, was composed and transmitted in secret for about three hundred years; and that is why it did not attain wide publicity. It is only in the Sādhana composed by Asaṅga[1] that we find a definite reference to the five Dhyāni Buddhas and their families, and it is for that reason not unreasonable to connect Asaṅga with the introduction of the very *Guhyasamājatantra* itself. The subsequent writers got only a glimpse of what filtered through the secret organizations. After the eighth century secrecy was no longer required, as the principles of Vajrayāna then were fully established and widely spread, through the teachings and mystic songs of the eighty-four Siddhapuruṣas.

The pantheon of the Northern Buddhists revolves round the

[1] Sādhana No. 159, in the *Sādhanamālā*.

PLATE III

ÀDI-BUDDHA VAJRADHARA

theory of the five Dhyāni Buddhas. The Buddhists believed that the world is composed of five elements, or Skandhas: Rūpa, Vedanā, Saṁjñā, Saṁskāra and Vijñāna; and these were deified in Vajrayāna in the form of the five Dhyāni Buddhas. In course of time these five Dhyāni Buddhas were regarded as primordial gods, and, therefore, Vajrayāna took more or less a polytheistic form. The priests were conscious of this defect, especially when they found all the six systems of Hindu philosophy setting up a monotheistic form. They tried to cure this defect by the theory of Vajradhara, that is, the Ādi or the primordial monotheistic god, to whom even the Dhyāni Buddhas owe their origin. The theory originated in the Nālandā monastery in about the tenth century. Thereafter a large number of images of Vajradhara must have been made in the different schools of art, as can be inferred from the numerous Vajradhara images which are to be found in the Nepal and Tibetan schools. Alexander Csoma de Koros places the introduction of this conception of Ādi-Buddha in Central India in the latter half of the tenth century.[1] It originated at Nālandā, according to him, in the beginning of the tenth century, and no mention of Ādi-Buddha is made by any writer before that time. Homage is paid to Ādi-Buddha in the shape of a flame of fire, which the priests consider as eternal, self-born and self-existent. It is said in the *Svayambhūpurāṇa* that the Ādi-Buddha first manifested himself in Nepal, in the form of a flame of fire, and Mañjuśrī erected a temple over it, in order to preserve the flame. This temple is known as the Svayambhū Caitya.[2]

The conception of Vajradhara in human form pre-supposes Ādi-Buddha, and, therefore, is later than the first half of the tenth century. Vajrasattva, being a regular development of Vajrapāṇi,

[1] J.A.S.B., Vol. II, 1833, pp. 57 ff. See also Bhattacharyya, 'Vajradhar vs. Vajrasattva,' in J.B.O.R.S., IX, pp. 114 ff.

[2] Oldfield, *Sketches from Nepal*, II, pp. 90, 156 ff., 188; *Hodgson's Essays*, pp. 115 ff.

the Bodhisattva emanating from Akṣobhya, is a little earlier, though the conceptions of Vajrasattva and Vajradhara are sometimes inextricably mixed up. In Vajrayāna Ādi-Buddha is regarded as the highest deity, the originator even of the Dhyāni Buddhas. When represented in human form, he begets the name of Vajradhara, and is conceived in two forms, single and yab-yum. When single he is bedecked in jewels and gaudy ornaments, sits in the Vajraparyaṅka attitude, carrying the Vajra in the right hand and the Ghaṇṭā in the left, the two hands being crossed against the breast in what is known as the Vajrahuṁkāra Mudrā. In yab-yum form he is the same as above described, with the difference that he is in this case locked in an embrace with his Śakti, whose name, according to Miss Getty, is Prajñāpāramitā. The Śakti is somewhat smaller in size, is richly dressed and bedecked in ornaments, carrying the Kartri in the right hand and the Kapāla in the left.[1]

But Vajradhara was not universally accepted as the Ādi-Buddha. When the theory of Ādi-Buddha was fully established, the Buddhists ranged themselves into many sects, as it were, holding different views regarding specific forms which the Ādi-Buddha should take. Some considered one among the five Dhyāni Buddhas as Ādi-Buddha; some acknowledged Vajrasattva as the Ādi-Buddha; and according to some the Bodhisattvas, Samantabhadra and Vajrapāṇi, were regarded as Ādi-Buddhas. Thus the cult of Ādi-Buddha was distributed amongst the different theories, which gave rise to as many different sects amongst the Tāntric Buddhists.

Dhyāni Buddhas

The Dhyāni Buddhas are a peculiar kind of Buddhas, who are not required to pass through the stage of a Bodhisattva. They have never been anything less nor more than a Buddha; they are

[1] Bhattacharyya, *Indian Buddhist Iconography*, p. xxviii.

PLATE IV

(*a*) AKṢOBHYA

(*b*) VAIROCANA

(*c*) LOCANĀ

(*d*) VAJRADHĀTVĪSVARĪ

PLATE V

(a) Amitābha

(b) Ratnasambhava

(c) Amoghasiddhi

always engaged in peaceful meditation and they voluntarily restrain themselves from the act of creation. To create is a duty of their emanations or the divine Bodhisattvas. The Dhyāni Buddhas are five in number, to which a sixth, Vajrasattva, is sometimes added. The theory of the five Dhyāni Buddhas was promulgated in about the third century A.D., for the first time in the *Guhyasamāja* and later on developed in the Tāntric Buddhism. It may be possible that the five Mudrās, which Buddha Śākyasiṁha made sacred by using on memorable occasions, and which were constantly represented in the Buddhistic figures of the different schools of art, gave rise to the five Dhyāni Buddhas. The Tāntric authorities, however, maintain that the five Dhyāni Buddhas took their origin from the theory of the eternity of the five Skandhas, or elements, which were held by Buddha to be the constituents of a being fused together by action. Vajrasattva, the sixth Dhyāni Buddha, was generally regarded as the priest of the five Dhyāni Buddhas, and is usually represented with the priestly symbols, the Vajra and Ghaṇṭā. He is an embodiment of the five Skandhas collectively, and undoubtedly a later incorporation into the pantheon. The five Dhyāni Buddhas are Vairocana, Akṣobhya, Ratnasambhava, Amitābha and Amoghasiddhi. When represented they appear all alike. But they vary in regard to the particular colour of their body and the different mystic poses exhibited in their hands, and according to their vehicles and recognition symbols. Every Dhyāni Buddha is represented in a sitting posture on a full-blown double lotus, the attitude being known as the meditative pose, in which he is required to sit cross-legged, the right foot crossing over and in front of the left, the soles of both feet turned upwards. The hand, which rests on the lap, is sometimes empty; but in most cases it carries a bowl; the head is bare and the hair curly, which radiates effulgence like a flame of fire, and the eyes are half-closed in token of meditation. The dress consists of an under-garment, reaching from the breast to the knees and tied by a scarf. The body is loosely covered by the habit of a monk, leaving the right arm bare. The Dhyāni Buddhas are generally represented on the four sides of a stūpa, which is the symbol of the Buddhist universe. Four out of the five face the four cardinal points; Vairocana, the deity of the inner shrine, being generally unrepresented. But when he is represented outside, he is assigned a place between Ratnasambhava and Akṣobhya. On the stūpa, Akṣobhya faces east; Ratnasambhava south, Amitābha west, and Amoghasiddhi north. Vairocana is supposed to reside in the heart, or the sanctum, of the stūpa. Occasionally Vairocana and Akṣobhya change places; and in this state they appear in the Dhyāni-Buddha-Maṇḍala, described in the *Guhyasamāja*.

These Dhyāni Buddhas are regarded as the progenitors of the different families of Buddhist gods and goddesses. They are assigned a Śakti each, through whom the families are brought into existence. The families are Dveṣa, Moha, Rāga, Cintāmaṇi and Samaya. The members of each family are required to show their origin by holding the figure of their parental Dhyāni Buddha on their heads.[1]

The colour, mudrā, vāhana and recognition symbol of the different Dhyāni Buddhas is shown in the following table:

NAME	COLOUR	MUDRĀ	VĀHANA	SYMBOL
Akṣobhya	Blue	Bhūsparśa	Elephant	Vajra
Vairocana	White	Dharmacakra	Dragon	Cakra
Amitābha	Red	Samādhi	Peacock	Lotus
Ratnasambhava	Yellow	Varada	Horse	Jewels
Amoghasiddhi	Green	Abhaya	Garuḍa	Viśvavajra

[1] *Indian Buddhist Iconography*, chap. I, pp. 1 ff.

PLATE VI

(*a*) PĀṆḌARĀ

(*b*) MĀMAKĪ

(*c*) ĀRYATĀRĀ

PLATE VII

(*a*) VAJRASATTVA IN YAB-YUM
(Front view)

(*b*) VAJRASATTVA

(*c*) VAJRASATTVA IN YAB-YUM
(Back view)

I. The Dveṣa Family

The Dveṣa family is presided over by Akṣobhya, who is represented in the Bhūmiṣparśa, or the earth-touching attitude. He is first mentioned as a Tathāgata in the smaller recension of the Amitāyus-sūtra, which was translated into Chinese between A.D. 384 and 417. His Śakti is Locanā; and his principal Bodhisattva is Vajrapāṇi. A large number of gods and goddesses emanate from Akṣobhya, and these constitute the Dveṣa family.

Amongst the gods emanating from Akṣobhya, Heruka, Hayagrīva and Yamāri are the chief. The blue colour of Akṣobhya is associated with terrible deities and gruesome rites in the Tantra. The deities emanating from Akṣobhya usually take a blue colour and they exhibit an awe-inspiring appearance, with distorted face, bare fangs, three eyes, protruding tongue, garland of severed heads and skulls, tiger's skin and ornaments of snakes.

1. HERUKA[1]

Amongst the members of the Dveṣa family Heruka is perhaps the most popular and the most powerful. He is assigned many Śaktis, and, as he is associated with the different Śaktis, his forms are distinctively called Buddhakapāla, Samvara, Vajraḍāka, Saptākṣara and Mahāmāyā. Independent Tantras, said to be delivered by Buddha in an assembly of the faithful, are ascribed to all these different forms of Heruka. When two-armed Heruka dances in the Ardhaparyaṅka attitude on a corpse, and carries the Vajra and the skull cup full of human blood in the two hands. The Khaṭvāṅga, surmounted by human skulls with flowing banner, hangs from the left shoulder like the sacred thread. In the two-armed form he is

[1] The descriptions of all these emanations have been summarized from the elaborate sādhanas in the *Sādhanamālā*. The same procedure is followed in the whole chapter. See also descriptions in *Indian Buddhist Iconography*.

sometimes associated with a Śakti, who closely embraces him and carries the Kartri and the Kapāla in her hands.

When four-armed he is also conceived in yab-yum and carries the Vajra, the sword, the Khaṭvāṅga and the jewel. When he is embraced by Citrasenā in yab-yum, he is called Buddhakapāla and carries the Khaṭvāṅga, the Kapāla, the Kartri and the Ḍamaru; and the pair is surrounded by twenty-four goddesses arranged in three circles.

When Heruka is associated with Vajravārāhī he is usually designated as Vajraḍāka, which also takes two different forms as Samvara and Saptākṣara. Samvara is two-armed, stands in the Ālīḍha attitude and tramples upon Kālaratri. He carries the Vajra and the Ghaṇṭā; while his Śakti Vajravārāhī shows the Vajra and the Kapāla full of blood. Saptākṣara, on the other hand, has three faces and six arms, though he is embraced by the same goddess, Vajravārāhī. He carries the Vajra, the Ghaṇṭā and a human skin in the three left hands, and the Kapāla, the Khaṭvāṅga and the Triśūla in the three right hands. His Śakti Vajravārāhī carries the same symbols as her master. The pair is surrounded by six deities, arranged in a circle.

When Heruka is associated with Vajrayoginī, who is generally known as Buddhaḍākinī, he has the name of Mahāmāyā. In this form Heruka has four arms and four faces, and dances in the Ardhaparyaṅka attitude. He carries in his four hands the Kapāla, the arrow, the Khaṭvāṅga and the bow. His Prajñā Buddhaḍākinī also shows the same symbols and is endowed with the same form as her master. The pair is surrounded by four goddesses in the four cardinal directions.

2. YAMĀRI

Yamāri is another god belonging to the Dveṣa family. Independent Tantras are devoted to his worship, and they relate to two different forms of Yamāri, red and blue. It is said that, in accordance with the different functions discharged by the deity, he gets different colours. For instance, in Śānti he is white and faces the east; in Pauṣṭika he is yellow and faces the north; in Vaśya he is red and faces the west; and in Ākarṣaṇa he is blue and faces the south, and so on. Of these, the red and blue forms are more popular; and this means that his worship was mostly performed with a view to enchanting men and women and to force them to submission and bring them to the worshipper. Yamāri may be worshipped singly, or in yab-yum in conjunction with the Śakti. He should have the head of a buffalo on his shoulders and should ride on a buffalo. The Tibetans relate a very interesting story regarding the origin of this fearful god. It is said that there was once a holy man, who lived in a cave in deep meditation for fifty years, after which he was to enter into Nirvāṇa. Just a few hours before the completion of this period, two robbers entered the cave with a stolen bull and slaughtered it there; but when they discovered the presence of the ascetic, a witness to their crime, they beheaded him. Immediately he was killed his body assumed the ferocious form of Yama, and, taking up the bull's head, he set it upon his headless shoulders. He then killed the two robbers, and drank their blood from the cup made out of their skulls. In his fiery and insatiable thirst for victims he threatened to de-populate the whole of Tibet. The Tibetans appealed to their tutelary deity Mañjuśrī, whereupon the latter assumed the fierce form of Yamāntaka, and defeated Yama in a sanguinary battle. This probably illustrates the popular belief that the buffalo is more powerful than the bull.

Yamāri in his red form is usually conceived as standing in the Pratyālīḍha attitude, and as carrying the Kapāla full of blood in the left hand and a white staff surmounted by a severed head in the right. He is decked in ornaments of snakes, has brown hair rising upwards, and wears a tiger's skin. The Śakti, who embraces him in yab-yum, also stands in the Pratyālīḍha attitude. She has two arms, garments of tiger's skin, and is intoxicated with wine.

Yamāri, when blue, may have either one face and two arms, or three faces and four arms, or three or six faces and six arms. When he is two-armed, he stands in the Pratyālīḍha attitude, and shows a staff surmounted by a Vajra in the right hand, and the raised index finger with a noose in the left hand placed against the breast. When three-faced and four-armed he is conceived in yab-yum in the embrace of the Śakti. He carries in his right hands the hammer and the sword; in the 'wo left the lotus and the jewel. When three-faced and six-armed he may also be represented singly; and in this form he carries the thunderbolt, the sword and the Mūṣala in the three right hands; and the goblin (Vetālī), the axe and the lasso in the three left. He may also have the sword, the Mudgara and the thunderbolt in the three right hands; and the Ghaṇṭā, the Vajrapāśa and the Mūṣala in the three left. In the second form he may have six faces and six legs, with the same weapons.

3. EKAJAṬĀ

Amongst the female members of the Dveṣa family, Ekajaṭā and Nairātmā may be cited as specimens. As is usual with the members of the Dveṣa family, both these goddesses have a blue form and they are terrible in appearance and awe-inspiring, with hair rising upwards in the shape of a flame of fire, canine teeth, garments of tiger's skin, thre bloodshot eyes and protruding tongue. Regarding Ekajaṭā said that her worship was introduced by Siddha Nāgārju one of the eighty-four Mahāsiddhas, in the middle of the se h century, from the country of of Bhoṭa or Tibet. The country of Bhoṭa was also known as Mahācīna, and this accounts for the name Mahācīna Tārā, which is given to the four-armed variety of Ekajaṭā. She was conceived in four different forms—as one-faced, having two, four or eight arms; and as twelve-faced with twenty-four arms. When two-armed, she is conceived as carrying the Kartri, or knife, in her

PLATE VIII

NAIRĀTMĀ

right hand and the Kapāla, or the skull cup, in the left. When four-armed, she carries the arrow and the sword in the two right hands and the bow and the skull in the two left. As Mahācīna Tārā, she carries the sword and the Kartri in the two right hands and the Utpala and the Kapāla in the two left. When eight-armed, she shows the sword, the arrow, the Vajra and the Kartri in the four right hands; and the bow, the Utpala, the Paraśu and the skull in the four left hands. When twelve-faced and twenty-four-armed, she gets the name of Vidyujjvālākarālī and tramples on four principal Hindu gods — Indra, Brahmā, Viṣṇu and Śiva. She carries the Khaḍga, Vajra, Cakra, jewel, Aṅkuśa, arrow, dart, Mudgara, Mūṣala, Kartri, Ḍamaru and rosary in the twelve right hands; and the bow, noose, Tarjanī, banner, mace, Triśūla, Caṣaka, Utpala, bell, Paraśu, severed head of Brahmā and Kapāla in the twelve left.

4. NAIRĀTMĀ

Nairātmā is another goddess who emanates from Akṣobhya. The word, Nairātmā, means soul-less, which is another name for Śūnya, in which the Bodhisattva merges on the attainment of Nirvāṇa. In Vajrayāna the conception of Śūnya took the form of a goddess in whose eternal embrace the Bodhisattva is said to remain in eternal bliss and happiness. Nairātmā gets the blue colour because the colour of Śūnya, according to Buddhist traditions, is the same as the colour of the sky.

Nairātmā is conceived as standing in Ardhaparyaṅka, in a dancing attitude on the chest of a corpse. She carries the Kartri in the right hand and the Kapāla in the left; and a Khaṭvāṅga hangs from the left shoulder. She is decked with the five auspicious symbols, or the Mudrās, viz. the torque, the bracelet, the girdle, the tiara and the armlets. Images of Nairātmā are extremely rare.

II. The Moha Family

The originator of the Moha family is Vairocana, who is usually conceived as sitting in the Vajraparyaṅka attitude, white in colour, and showing the Dharmacakra Mudrā. His recognition symbol is the Cakra, or the disc, and his Vāhana is a pair of dragons. His place is in the middle of the stūpa, and therefore he is not usually represented outside the stūpa; but exceptions to this rule are occasionally to be found, when he is given a place in the corner between Akṣobhya in the east and Ratnasambhava in the south. His Bodhisattva is Samantabhadra and his Śakti is Vajradhātvīśvarī, through whom he brings forth the members of his family. Amongst the members of the family, Mārīcī and Vajravārāhī may be cited as examples.

1. Mārīcī

Mārīcī is invoked by the Lamas of Tibet at the advent of the morning, showing her connexion with the sun. Like the Hindu sun god, she also has a chariot; but the chariot of Mārīcī is drawn by seven pigs, while that of the sun is drawn by seven horses. The sun has a charioteer in Aruṇa, who has no legs: while the charioteer in the case of Mārīcī is Rāhu, who has only a head and nothing else. Mārīcī is conceived in six different forms. She may have one, three, five or six faces, and two, eight, ten or twelve arms. She is generally accompanied by her four attendants, Vartālī, Vadālī, Varālī and Varāhamukhī, and is recognized by her sow face and the seven pigs that run her chariot. The needle and thread are her characteristic symbols, by which she is said to sew up the mouths and the eyes of the wicked. Images of Mārīcī are rather common in India. In her two-armed form of Aśokakāntā she is seen in sculptures as an attendant of Khadiravanī Tārā, who is an emanation of Amoghasiddhi. Among the other varieties of Mārīcī, the form with three faces and eight arms is extensively found in sculptures.

PLATE IX

MĀRICI

When two-armed, Mārīcī has the name of Aśokakāntā, and in this form she holds the bough of an Aśoka tree in the left hand and exhibits the Varadamudrā in the right hand. She is decorated with bright jewels, wears white garments, and is conceived as standing on a pig of golden colour.

The second, Ārya-mārīcī, is identical in all other respects with Aśokakāntā, and can only be distinguished by the symbols which she bears in her hands. Instead of the Aśoka bough and Varada pose, Ārya-mārīcī carries the needle and thread.

When three-faced and eight-armed, Mārīcī has the name of Mārīcī-picuvā, is yellow in colour, wears red garments, and is decked in various ornaments. Her three faces display three different sentiments. The middle displays amour, and is yellow in colour; the left face is distorted sow-like, is blue in colour, and displays wrath, with bared fangs and protruding lips. The right face is red in colour, glows in heavenly splendour, and displays the sentiment of Śānta. In her six hands she holds the needle and thread in the first pair, the elephant-goad and the noose in the second pair, the bow and arrow in the third, and the thunderbolt and the Aśoka flowers in the fourth. She is accompanied by four goddesses, situated in the four cardinal directions.

When three-faced and twelve-armed, she may be called the Ubhayavarāhānana Mārīcī, because her two faces, to the right and the left of the principal one, are depicted sow-like, unlike any other three-faced form of Mārīcī. She stands in the Ālīḍha attitude, is clad in tiger's skin, has red complexion, bejewelled head-dress, a red scarf, and is decked in jewellery. The principal face smiles with delight, is peaceful in appearance, and displays the sentiment of amour. The face to the left is red, while the right has very great effulgence, like the Saindhava salt. Homage is paid to her by a deity carrying the Vajra and the Mudgara in the left, and by Purandara, carrying the Vajra and the noose in the right, hand. In her six left hands she shows the

Tarjanī against the breast, the Aśoka bough, the Aṅkuśa, the Kapāla, the severed head of Brahmā and the vessel. The six right hands carry the needle, the Aṅkuśa, the Bhiṇḍipāla, the sword, the Kartri and the staff surmounted by a Vajra. She tramples under her feet the principal Hindu gods, such as Viṣṇu, Śiva and Brahmā.

When five-faced and ten-armed, she has four legs and a white colour like the colour of the Dhyāni Buddha Vairocana. Of the five faces, the principal face is white, the one to the right is blue, the other to the left is red and distorted, sow-like. The face behind is green, and the one above is yellow, and bears the Triśikhā and the crown of chignon (Jaṭā). The five right hands hold the sun, the thunderbolt, the arrow, the goad and the needle. The five left hands carry the moon, the bow, the Aśoka bough, the noose with the Tarjanī and the thread. She also tramples under her feet the four Hindu gods, Indra, Śiva, Viṣṇu and Brahmā.

When six-faced and twelve armed, she gets three different names—Vajradhātvīśvarī Mārīcī, Oḍiyāna Mārīcī and Vajravetālī. These three different varieties are due to slight differences in weapons that are held in their hands. They are all endowed with six faces and twelve arms. The first five faces are respectively red, blue, green, yellow and white. The face on the top is distorted sow-like, and has a blue colour. She stands in the Ālīḍha attitude and presents a terrifying appearance, with three eyes in each face, protruding tongue, bared fangs, ornaments of serpents, and a garment of tiger's skin. Vajradhātvīśvarī carries in her six right hands the sword, the Mūṣala, the arrow, the goad, the Vajra and the Paraśu; and in her six left shows the noose (occasionally with Tarjanī), the Kapāla, the Aśoka bough, the severed head of Brahmā, the bow and the Triśūla. Oḍiyāna Mārīcī holds the Cakra in the right instead of the goad, and the Khaṭvāṅga-Kapāla in one of the left hands, instead of the Kapāla only. Vajravetālī in one of her right hands holds the crossed double thunderbolt, or the Cakra, and in one of the left the noose instead of the Kapāla or the Khatvāṅga-Kapāla. The other hands carry the same weapons in all the three cases.

2. VAJRAVĀRĀHĪ

Vajravārāhī is another important member of the Moha family. She is so called because she has an excrescence near the right ear, which resembles the face of a sow; and this is evident from the epithet Vajraghoṇā, which is usually applied to her. The union of Vajravārāhī with Heruka is the subject matter of the two popular Buddhist Tantras, namely the *Cakrasamvaratantra* and the *Vajravārāhītantra*. She is described in the Sādhanas as the first queen of the god Śrī Heruka. She is also called a Ḍākinī, which in Buddhist Tantra signifies any goddess who may be associated with the male gods in yab-yum. She is described also as Vairocanakulodbhavā, or belonging to the Vairocana family.

Vajravārāhī is conceived in three different forms. The first two are one-faced and two-armed, while the third is four-armed. In all forms she is terrible in appearance, with three eyes, dishevelled hair, the six Mudrās, the Pratyālīḍha attitude, and a garland of severed heads. She is entirely nude, and dances on a corpse. She is surrounded by four deities of the Maṇḍala, viz. Ḍākinī, Lāmā, Khaṇḍarohā and Rūpiṇī. In the first form she stands in the Pratyālīḍha attitude, and shows in the right hand the Vajra, with Tarjanī and the Kapāla in the left, the Khaṭvāṅga hanging from her left shoulder.

In the second form she dances in the Ardhaparyaṅka attitude on a corpse lying on its breast, and carries the Kartri in a menacing attitude in the right hand, and the Kapāla, full of blood, in the left. The Khaṭvāṅga, as usual, hangs from the left shoulder. This variety of Vajravārāhī is invoked widely in the rite of bewitching men and women, and her worship is very popular in modern days in Nepal and other Buddhist countries.

The third, or four-armed form, of Vajravārāhī is known as Ārya-Vajravārāhī, and carries in the two right hands the Vajra and the elephant goad, and in the two left the Kapāla with the Tarjanī and the noose. She is one-faced, three-eyed, and appears terrible, with contortions of the brows, the adamantine excrescence and the protruding tongue, teeth and belly. She stands in the Ālīḍha attitude on a corpse, unlike the other forms of Vajravārāhī, and the Khaṭvāṅga hangs from her left shoulder, as usual.

III. The Rāga Family

The progenitor of the Rāga family is Amitābha, who is usually represented as sitting in the meditative pose and as showing the Samādhi-mudrā in his two hands, which are placed on the lap, one over the other, with the palms of both hands facing upwards. His colour is red, his recognition symbol is the lotus, and his Vāhana is a pair of elephantṣ. When represented on the stūpa, his chapel appears on the west. His Bodhisattva is Padmapāṇi and his Śakti is Pāṇḍarā, through whom he brings forth the members of his family.

1. LOKEŚVARA

Amongst the members of the Rāga family, Lokeśvara, or Avalokiteśvara, is the chief, who is undoubtedly the most popular deity of the Vajrayāna pantheon, because he is the very embodiment of compassion, to whom as many as one hundred and eight forms are attributed. Amongst these the two forms, Khasarpaṇa and Siṁhanāda, may be cited as examples.

Khasarpaṇa is two-armed and one-faced, and carries the lotus in the left hand and shows the Varadamudrā in the right. He has a genuinely peaceful appearance, and is endowed with various auspicious marks. From his right hand flows the stream of nectar, which is received by Sūcimukha, the goblin, who stands below with an uplifted face, a protruding belly, and an emaciated appearance. He is accompanied by four deities, Tārā, Sudhana-

PLATE X

SIMHANADA LOKESVARA

kumāra, Bhṛkuṭī and Hayagrīva, in the four cardinal directions. Tārā is green. With her right hand she makes blossom the lotus held in her left. Sudhanakumāra has his two hands joined against his breast and carries a book under his left armpit. Bhṛkuṭī is four-armed, has matted hair, and carries the staff with three horns and the Kamaṇḍalu in her two left hands. Of the two right, one is raised in the attitude of bowing while the other carries the rosary. Hayagrīva has red complexion, a stunted appearance, and a protruding belly, and his hair rises upwards in the shape of a flame of fire. He has a snake as his sacred thread, and his face is recognized by a moustache of a deep brown colour. He is clad in a tiger's skin and his appearance is awe-inspiring. His right hand exhibits the mudrā of bowing; and in the left he carries the staff as a weapon.

Siṁhanāda, the other form of Avalokiteśvara, is widely worshipped as a curer of all forms of disease. He is conceived as of white complexion, with three eyes, the crown of chignon and a tiger's skin as garment. He has no ornaments, is mounted on a lion, and sits in the attitude of princely ease. To his right there is a white trident entwined by a white snake; and to his left is a lotus-bowl full of fragrant flowers. From his left hand rises a white lotus, on which a fiery white sword is placed.

2. KURUKULLĀ

Amongst the goddesses emanating from the Dhyāni Buddha Amitābha, Kurukullā may be cited as an example. Kurukullā is said to confer success in the Tāntric rite of Vaśīkaraṇa, or betwitching. If her mantra is muttered ten thousand times any man can be bewitched, thirty thousand will be sufficient for subduing a minister, and one lakh for a king. Her mantra is also a charm against snake bites; and it has the power to extract poison from patients bitten by a snake. Kurukullā is worshipped in four different forms, with two, four, six or eight arms. When two-armed she is white in appearance, sits in the Vajraparyaṅka attitude, and carries the rosary and the bowl of lotuses. She displays the sentiment of passionate love and compassion, and wears the ornaments of eight snakes. When four-armed she has a red complexion, red garments, red ornaments and a seat of red lotus. She shows the Abhayamudrā and the arrow in the two right hands, and the bow and the red lotus in the two left. She sits in the Vajraparyaṅka attitude, and under her lotus seat appear Kāmadeva and his wife riding on Rāhu. Sometimes she fits an arrow to the bow and is ready to strike. She may have another form, which is known as Oḍiyāna Kurukullā, when endowed with four arms. This form is terrible in appearance, with the garland of heads, five skulls on the head, protruding teeth and tongue, garments of tiger's skin, and brown hair rising on her head in the shape of a flame of fire. Out of four arms the principal pair is engaged in drawing to the full the flowery bow, charged with an arrow of red lotus. The second pair holds a goad of flowers and the red lotus. In this form she sits in the Ardhaparyaṅka attitude on a corpse.

When six-armed she exhibits in the first pair of hands the Trailokyavijayamudrā, in the second pair the goad and the red lotus, and in the third the full-drawn bow with an arrow. She exhibits the sentiment of amour, is youthful in appearance, and clad in red garments and red upper garments, and wears all kinds of ornaments. She is red in colour, and sits on a lotus in the Vajraparyaṅka attitude.

When eight-armed, she is represented as mild, youthful and compassionate. She is red in complexion, and sits in the Vajraparyaṅka attitude. She displays the Trailokyavijayamudrā in her first pair of hands, the full-drawn bow and the arrow in the second pair, the goad and the noose in the third pair, the Varadamudrā and the Utpala in the fourth pair. She is accompanied by Prasannatārā in the east, Niṣpannatārā in the south, Jayatārā in the west, and the Karṇatārā in the north.

PLATE XI

JAMBHALA

IV. The Cintāmaṇi Family

At the head of the Cintāmaṇi family is the Dhyāni Buddha, Ratnasambhava, who is usually conceived as yellow in colour and as exhibiting the Varadamudrā, or the gift-bestowing pose. His Vāhana is a pair of horses and his recognition symbol is the jewel. When represented on the stūpa he occupies a chapel towards the south. Not many deities emanate from him, nor is he regarded as an Ādi-Buddha by any of the numerous Buddhist sects. His Bodhisattva is Ratnapāṇi and his Śakti is Māmakī, through whom he brings forth the members of his family. Amongst the deities belonging to his family Jambhala, the god of wealth, and Vasudhārā, the goddess of plenty, are the chief, and may be cited as examples.

1. JAMBHALA

As an emanation of Ratnasambhava he may be conceived as single, as also in yab-yum. When single, Jambhala is of golden complexion and carries the mongoose in the left hand and the citron in the right. The mongoose is supposed to be the receptacle of all gems, and when Jambhala presses the two sides of the mongoose it vomits forth the riches. By noticing this mongoose in actual representations it is easy to recognize the possessor to be Jambhala. When represented in yab-yum, he sits on the moon, placed on a double conventional lotus of eight petals. He wears all sorts of ornaments, a garland of yellow lotuses, and is locked in embrace with Vasudhārā. His complexion is golden yellow; he has a protruding belly, and he carries the mongoose and the citron in his left and right hands respectively. The eight petals of the lotus are occupied by eight Yakṣas, who are also associated with their respective Śaktis in yab-yum. The Śakti, Vasudhārā, is yellow in complexion, and carries the ears of corn and shows the Varadamudrā in her two hands.

Jambhala has another fierce form in Ucchuṣma Jambhala, who

is conceived as standing in the Pratyālīḍha attitude, with his left leg stretched forward on the forehead of Kubera, the Hindu god of wealth; while the right, which is somewhat bent, tramples upon his two legs. He has a terrible appearance, with a protruding belly, bared fangs and ornaments of snakes. He holds the Kapāla, full of blood, against his breast, and looks eagerly towards it with his three eyes. The left hand carries the mongoose, near the thigh.

2. VASUDHĀRĀ

Amongst the female members of the Cintāmaṇi family Vasudhārā is noteworthy. Vasudhārā is the goddess of plenty, and is worshipped for various boons. She is fully decked in ornaments, and is invariably accompanied by her confidants. Her complexion is always yellow, like the colour of Ratnasambhava, and she carries in her left hand ears of corn placed on a vessel which showers gems; while the right hand exhibits the Varadamudrā. Vasudhārā is very popular with the Hindus, who worship her widely, and there are many Hindu Tāntric works in which the Vasudhārā cult is inculcated.

V. THE SAMAYA FAMILY

At the head of the Samaya family is the Dhyāni Buddha, Amoghasiddhi; and a tolerably large number of deities emanates from him. His left hand lies open on his lap, and the right exhibits the Abhaya-mudrā, or the attitude of assurance. When represented, his colour is green and he always faces north in the stūpa. His Vāhana is a pair of Garuḍas and his recognition symbol is Viśvavajra, or the conventional double thunderbolt. Sometimes a serpent with seven hoods forms the background, while the expanded hoods appear like an umbrella. In front of his shrine, therefore, is found a small square pit, which represents the tank in which the serpent resides. His Bodhisattva is Viśvapāṇi and his consort is Āryatārā, through whom he brings the members of his family into

PLATE XII

PARṆAŚAVARĪ

existence. All the members of his family, it may be remarked, are females, no male emanation of this Dhyāni Buddha being known except Viśvapāṇi; nor is he known to have been regarded ever as the Ādi-Buddha by any of the sects. Amongst the emanations of Amoghasiddhi, Khadiravaṇī Tārā and Parṇaśavarī may be cited as examples.

1. KHADIRAVAṆĪ TĀRĀ

Khadiravaṇī is conceived as green in colour, like her parental Dhyāni Buddha, and is endowed with one face and two arms, which show the Varadamudrā in the right and the Utpala in the left. She is generally accompanied with two attendant deities, Aśokāntā Mārīcī and Ekajaṭā.

2. PARṆAŚAVARĪ

Parṇaśavarī, the second deity emanating from Amoghasiddhi, is also green. The mantra assigned to her designates her as a Piśācī and as Sarvamāripraśamanī, or the destroyer of all kinds of epidemics. It is very probable that in times of epidemics, such as cholera, plague or smallpox, Parṇaśavarī was invoked and worshipped, in the same way as Rakṣākālī is worshipped in Indian villages in modern days, to prevent and ward off epidemics. Parṇaśavarī is endowed with three faces, with three eyes in each, and six arms. Her right and left faces are blue and white respectively. In her three right hands she carries the Vajra, Paraśu and the arrow; and in the three left the bow, the cluster of leaves and the Tarjanī with the noose. Her face is depicted with an angry laugh, and her hair is tied up above. She is in the fullness of youth, is decked in a tiger's skin, wears an apron of leaves, and tramples under her feet various diseases and pestilences. In the images of Parṇaśavarī discovered in East Bengal, two divinities are represented, to her right and left, as flying away in opposite directions in terror to escape the wrath of the principal goddess. They are Hayagrīva—the Hindu god of fever; and Śītalā—the

Hindu goddess of smallpox. The prostrate figures under the feet in these images represent the diseases and pestilences in human shape. The figure under the right leg, apparently, is a man attacked with smallpox, as we can judge from the circular marks all over his body. The other figure, under her left foot, is probably attacked with some fatal disease.

CHAPTER XIV

INFLUENCE OF BUDDHIST TĀNTRISM ON HINDUISM

THE Tantras of the Hindus and Buddhists alike have incurred almost universal hatred and neglect at the hand of the Indologist. But whether the Tantras are altogether divested of great possibilities in future is a question which requires a careful and considerate handling. The Tantras are a product of a period between the seventh and twelfth centuries A.D., though many Hindu Tantras have been written even later, right up to the last century. It is possible to declare, without fear of contradiction, that the Buddhists were the first to introduce the Tantras into their religion, and that the Hindus borrowed them from the Buddhists in later times, and that it is idle to say that later Buddhism was an outcome of Śaivaism. A study of the Tantras has revealed these facts, and it is likely to yield much historical information in the course of time, because we must remember that a great volume of the history of India, especially Eastern India, is buried in this literature.

With regard to mutual interchange of deities it can be definitely said that the Hindus developed a pantheon in a very remote age, and, with the rise of Buddhism and Jainism, their followers had to borrow some of these Hindu deities for their pantheons. Though in the earlier period both Buddhism and Jainism exploited Hindu gods, the Buddhist pantheon was commonly ransacked by Hinduism and Jainism in the later and more promiscuous Tāntric age. We do not know how far the Jainas were influenced by the Buddhist Tāntrism, because we do not find a regular Tāntric literature in Jainism, as we find in Hinduism. It is, therefore, necessary to institute a comparative inquiry into the relative priority, or otherwise, of the Hindu and Buddhist Tantras, and this can be best accomplished by taking up the origin of certain deities common to both the systems.

Let us take, for example, the instance of the Hindu deity, Tārā, who is included in the group of the ten Mahāvidyā goddesses. These goddesses are personifications of certain mantras or Vidyās, popularly known as Siddhamantras, as they are reputed to bestow perfection on those who constantly mutter them one hundred thousand times. The ten Mahāvidyā goddesses are: Kālī, Tārā, Ṣoḍaśī, Bhuvaneśvarī, Bhairavī, Chinnamastā, Dhūmāvatī, Bagalā, Mātaṅgī and Kamalā.[1] A mantra is attached to each of these ten deities, and, according to changes in the order of the letters in the mantra, new forms of the same deity spring forth into existence. The mantra of Tārā, according to the Hindus, is Hrīṁ Strīṁ Hūṁ Phaṭ, which gives rise to seven more deities, according as the four syllables of the mantra are recited in different orders or sequence. These seven deities, who are regarded as seven different forms of the same deity Tārā, are named as Ugrā, Mahogrā, Vajrā, Kālī, Sarasvatī, Kāmeśvarī and Bhadrakālī.[2] The table at top of the next page shows the name and the mantra of each.

From the above it is not difficult to imagine that all the seven deities mentioned above represent seven different forms of the original deity, Tārā, who is one of the ten Mahāvidyās. If the

[1] *Tantrasāra*, Bengali ed. (Vasumati, 5th ed.), p. 360.

काली तारा महाविद्या षोडशी भुवनेश्वरी ।
भैरवी छिन्नमस्ता च विद्या धूमावती तथा ॥
बगला सिध्दविद्या च मातङ्गी कमलात्मिका ।
एता दशमहाविद्याः सिध्दविद्याः प्रकीर्तिताः ॥

[2] तारा चोग्रा महोग्रा च वज्रा काली सरस्वती ।
कामेश्वरी भद्रकाली इत्यष्टौ तारिणी स्मृता ॥

Tantrasāra, op. cit., p. 328.

Tārā	ह्रीँ	स्त्रीँ	हूँ	फट्
Ugrā	स्त्रीँ	ह्रीँ	हूँ	फट्
Mahogrā	हूँ	स्त्री	ह्रीँ	फट्
Vajrā	हूँ	ह्रीँ	स्त्रीँ	फट्
Kālī	ह्रीँ	स्त्रीँ	फट्	हूँ
Sarasvatī	स्त्रीँ	ह्रीँ	फट्	हूँ
Kāmeśvarī	ह्रीँ	हूँ	स्त्रीँ	फट्
Bhadrakālī	स्त्रीँ	हूँ	ह्रीँ	फट्

origin of Tārā is Hindu, then all the seven deities should be considered also Hindu; but if Tārā is Buddhist, it is to be admitted that the different varieties of the same deity should also be Buddhist in origin. This question, therefore, leads us to a discussion of the origin of the Hindu deity, Tārā.

In many Tāntric works of the Hindus Tārā is described. The *Tārātantra*, the *Tantrasāra*, the *Mahācīnācāratantra*, are among the many that may be cited in this connexion. The *Tantrasāra*[1] calls the deity Tāriṇī, or Tārā, and quotes the ritual from an earlier work, namely the *Bhairavatantra*. Tārā is described as standing in the Pratyālīḍha attitude, dark in complexion, wearing a garland of severed heads, short in stature, with a protruding belly and a tiger's skin round the loins, youthful in appearance and decked in five Mudrās. She is four-armed, her tongue protrudes, and she presents an awe-inspiring appearance; and is regarded as the bestower of all boons. She carries the sword and knife in the two right hands, and the severed head and the Utpala (blue lotus) in the two left hands. She has one chignon on her head, which is brown in colour and glistens with splendour, and is adorned with Akṣobhya.

[1] *Tantrasāra*, op. cit., p. 315.

Tārā is here described as decked in five Mudrās, as Ekajaṭā (one-chignoned), and as holding the figure of Akṣobhya on her crown. What the five Mudrās are, why the deity is designated as Ekajaṭā, and why there is the figure of Akṣobhya on her crown, are the three questions which cannot be satisfactorily explained in accordance with Hindu traditions. In the *Tantrasāra* an attempt has been made to explain the five Mudrās in a very crude manner. According to this work, the five Mudrās represent the five skulls which form part of the tiara worn on the head.[1] But this explanation does not seem to be convincing, because the tiara usually worn by the Tāntric deities of fierce nature always consists of five skulls, suspended by means of strings made of human bones, and attached together by means of four transverse lines. Therefore, if we accept the meaning as given in the *Tantrasāra*, it will be difficult to explain the four Mudrās or six Mudrās with which Tāntric deities are usually adorned.

Why Tārā should be designated as Ekajaṭā, or why she should have one chignon, is not explained in Hindu Tāntric works, and the authors never even considered that an explanation was necessary. With regard to the figure of Akṣobhya on the crown, the *Toḍalatantra*, quoted in the edition of the *Tārātantra*, attempts to offer a solution. There it is said that when the churning of the ocean was being done by the Devas and Asuras, a fatal poison came out which terrified all gods and goddesses. Because the god, Ŝiva, knew no terror (or kṣobha), and drank up the whole poison, he was called Akṣobhya, in whose company Mahāmāyā, or Tāriṇī, always revels.[2]

[1] op. cit., p. 315: पट्टिकाचतुष्टयान्वितकपालपञ्चकभूषितामित्यर्थः ।

But the ornament is nothing but the Cakrī, or the tiara of the Buddhists, which is one of the five Mudrās. See below.

[2] cf. समुद्रमथने देवि कालकूटं समुत्थितम् ।
सर्वे देवाश्च देव्यश्च महाक्षोभमवाप्नुयुः ॥
क्षोभादिरहितं यस्मात् पीतं हालाहलं विषम् ।

This explanation is ridiculous, to say the least, and indicates the unreliability of the Hindu Tāntric literature and its authors. Anyone who is acquainted with the classification of the Buddhist deities, in accordance with the five Dhyāni Buddhas, will be able to appreciate the absurdity and the hollowness of this explanation. The Hindus have no Ekajaṭā, but they have a Tārā, who is known as a form of Ekajaṭā. They have a variety of Mudrās, but none can be employed as an ornament. No other deity of the Hindus is known to have the figure of Akṣobhya or any other deity on the crown. None of the three points raised, therefore, is satisfactorily explained in accordance with Hindu tradition.

But when we turn to Buddhist Tāntric literature for a solution of these difficulties, we find a satisfactory explanation of all the three points stated above. In the Buddhist pantheon there is a powerful goddess, who is known as Ekajaṭā, and at least eight Sādhanas, devoted to her worship, are preserved in the *Sādhanamālā* of the Buddhists. Ekajaṭā is a fierce divinity and has several forms, from two-armed to sixteen-armed, and from one-faced to twelve-faced; and her different forms are differently named as Ugratārā, Mahācīnatārā, Vidyujjvālākarālī, Ārya-Ekajaṭā and Śukla-Ekajaṭā. Out of these the form of Buddhist Ekajaṭā, known as Mahācīnatārā, has the same appearance as that of the Hindu deity, Tārā.

As regards the second point of the ornament of the five Mudrās, the Buddhist Tantras also offer a solution. They recognize a set of six Mudrās, or ornaments, all made out of human bones, representing the six Pāramitās,[1] and, according as

अतएव महेशानि अक्षोभ्यः परिकीर्तितः ॥
तेन सार्द्धं महामाया तारिणी रमते सदा ॥

[1] *Sādhanamālā*, p. 494.

कण्ठिकारुचकं रत्नकुण्डलं भस्मसूत्रकम् ।
षट् वै पारमिता एता मुद्रारूपेण योजितः ॥

the one or the other of the six is dropped, the deities are described as decked in five Mudrās or four Mudrās. A large number of Buddhist deities are described as decked in ornaments of these Mudrās, numbering from four to six. Evidently, there were several enumerations of six Mudrās, which were not definitely fixed because the different Tantras had different enumerations. The following, among others, were included in the series of six Mudrās—(1) the torque, (2) bracelets, (3) ear-rings, (4) ashes, (5) the sacred thread, (6) the tiara, (7) the girdle, and (8) the jewels. When a deity is described as decked in five Mudrās, any five among the eight enumerated above are selected, in accordance with the traditions current amongst each school; and the five are presided over by the five Dhyāni Buddhas. Thus Akṣobhya is the presiding deity of the tiara; Amitābha of the ear-rings; Ratnasambhava of the torque; Vajrocana of the bracelets; and Amoghasiddhi of the girdle.[1]

Thus, though to the Hindus the five Mudrās may appear to be strange and in a way unintelligible, which fact is amply borne out by the attempt at their elucidation in the *Tantrasāra*, the Mudrās[2] as ornaments were not unknown to the Buddhists. They knew how many Mudrās could be applied in the form of ornaments; they knew their precise meaning, and their precise position in the different parts of the body, and could enumerate the different Dhyāni Buddhas associated with each of the five Mudrās.

Now, with regard to the third point, of having a figure of Akṣobhya on the crown of Tārā, it is also to be pointed out that an explanation of this phenomenon can come only from the Buddhist sources. It is absurd to believe in the mode of explanation suggested in the Hindu Tantras, especially in the

[1] See ibid., p. 475, lines 1–4. In other schools the ornaments differ.

[2] The word Mudrā has various meanings. It may mean a coin, a token, a stamp, an appetiser (for more drink), and the woman (as in Mahāmudrā), a Śakti, and so forth.

Toḍalatantra referred to previously, that it is the figure of Śiva which appears on the crown of Tārā: because Śiva is without terror (kṣobha), and therefore Akṣobhya. If that be so, why should other Śaiva deities not show the same miniature of Śiva on the crown? Why is it, then, that we do not come across any such miniature figure on the crown of any other deity in the Hindu pantheon? Those who are acquainted with the rudiments of Buddhist iconography know perfectly well that all deities of the Buddhist pantheon are divided generally into five classes,[1] as emanations of the five Dhyāni Buddhas: Amitābha, Akṣobhya, Ratnasambhava, Vairocana and Amoghasiddhi. The deities emanating from the different Dhyāni Buddhas form five families, as it were, and are required to show their origin by holding the miniature figures of their parental Dhyāni Buddha on the crown. When these emanated deities are represented in stone or metal or paintings, they show the miniature of their parental Dhyāni Buddha on their head. Thus Lokeśvara, Mahābala, Kurukullā emanate from Amitābha; Caṇḍaroṣaṇa, Heruka, Vajraḍāka emanate from Akṣobhya; Mārīcī, Uṣṇīṣavijayā, Sitātapatrā Aparājitā from Vairocana; Khadiravaṇī Tārā, Parṇaśavarī, Mahāmāyūrī from Amoghasiddhi; Jambhala, Vasudhārā, etc., from Ratnasambhava; and they show on the crown a small figure of their parental Buddha. Thus when Tārā is described as having the figure of Akṣobhya on the crown, it is easy to recognize the goddess as an emanation of the Dhyāni Buddha Akṣobhya, or, technically speaking, as belonging to the family of Akṣobhya and not of the Hindu Mahādeva, because he has no kṣobha, or terror.

From the above it is sufficiently clear that the character of the Hindu deity Tārā is thoroughly Buddhist, and therefore the deity must be of Buddhist origin. It has been already pointed out that the form of Ekajaṭā known as Mahācīnatārā amongst the

[1] Bhattacharyya, *Indian Buddhist Iconography*, foreword, p. vii, and the classification of the Buddhist Divinities in the body of the book.

Buddhists, is the true equivalent of the Hindu deity Tārā. Several Sādhanas in the *Sādhanamālā* describe the form of Mahācīnatārā, and the description given in verse by one Śāśvatavajra,[1] a Buddhist Tāntric author, materially conforms to the description (Dhyāna) generally current amongst the Hindus. One who will take pains to compare the two descriptions will be surprised to see their identity in both form and spirit; and the Hindu description to be an outcome of the Buddhist description. As is usual with them, the Buddhists composed their verses in ungrammatical Sanskrit, and when they were incorporated into Hinduism they took a strictly grammatical form and their language became chaste and elegant.

It has already been said that one of the many descriptions of Mahācīnatārā was composed by Śāśvatavajra, whose time is not definitely known; but as his name appears in a MS. which bears a date corresponding to A.D. 1165, his time cannot be later than the latter part of the eleventh century; but, fortunately for us, there is another clue which may determine the time of the introduction of the deity Ekajaṭā in India. With regard to the introduction of the worship of Ekajaṭā, it is said that it was Nāgārjuna who was instrumental in introducing her worship from the country of Bhoṭa;[2] and if we are to rely on this statement we must regard the deity Ekajaṭā to be of an entirely foreign origin. The time of Nāgārjuna is roughly the middle of the seventh century. Nāgārjuna was the guru of Śabaripā and the disciple of Sarahapā,[3] all three being included in the list of the eighty-four Mahāsiddhas. Nāgārjuna was one of the earliest writers on

[1] op. cit., pp. 210 and 211. कृतिः शाश्वतवज्रस्य सेयं मेधाप्रसाधनी ।

[2] op. cit., p. 267. एकजटासाधनं समासम् । आर्यनागार्जुनपादैर्भोटेषु उध्दृतम् ॥ The Ekajaṭā mentioned in the *Guhyasamāja* seems to be different, because the mantras in the two cases do not agree.

[3] See supra, p. 68.

Tāntric Buddhism and composed many works, the translations of which are now preserved in the pages of the Tibetan Tangyur.

The origin of Tārā, therefore, is neither Hindu nor Buddhist; but it is of Tibetan extraction. Not only the deity is foreign, but also her worship and the practices connected therewith are foreign. The evidences of the Hindu Tantras also point to the same direction. In the *Tārātantra*, for instance, we read of Bhairavī wishing to know from her consort the way in which Buddha and Vaśiṣṭha obtained Siddhi. Bhairava in reply said that by muttering the mantra of Ugratārā Buddha and Vaśiṣṭha obtained Siddhi; Mahādeva became the Lord of the world; Durvāsā, Vyāsa, Vālmīki, Bhāradvāja and others became great poets; and Bhīṣma, Arjuna and other Kṣattriyas became great conquerors.[1]

In the *Rudrayāmala*[2] it is said that Vaśiṣṭha, being unable to obtain Siddhi even after years of mutterings and severe austerities, at last pronounced a curse on the deity. She, thereupon, appeared before him, and told him that by these austerities it was impossible to attain Siddhi, but it would be easy of attainment if he went to Mahācīna, in the country of the Buddhists and the land of the Atharvaveda. Vaśiṣṭha thereafter repaired to Cīnabhūmi, where Buddha was residing and was indulging in all sorts of loathsome practices. Vaśiṣṭha was horrified to witness the scene, and appealed to Buddha to allay his doubts, and ultimately grant him the cherished Siddhi. He asked many questions regarding Buddha's use of wine and meat, and the presence of the women, entirely without dress, drinking blood and wine and behaving like drunkards, and wanted to know why Buddha associated himself with these women. Buddha was not perturbed at these direct questions, but gave him a lecture on the duties of Kaulas, and explained to him their mysteries and utility, and acquainted him with the secret rites and practices connected therewith. Vaśiṣṭha

[1] loc. cit., pp. 1–2.

[2] See *Tārātantra* (V.R.S. ed.), app., p. 23.

was fully convinced and soon followed the ways of Buddha, and eventually attained final liberation by an unrestrained use of the five Makāras. This is evident from the following verse:

एतच्छ्रुत्वा गुरोर्वाक्यं स्मृत्वा देवीं सरस्वतीम् ।
मदिरासाधनं कर्त्तुं जगाम कुलमण्डपे ॥
मद्यं मांसं तथा मत्स्यं मुद्रां मैथुनमेव च ।
पुनः पुनः साधयित्वा पूर्णयोगी बभूव सः ॥ [1]

Again in the *Brahmayāmala* the same story is repeated, with slight modifications. It is there recorded that Vaśiṣṭha, after coming to Mahācīna, became frightened and disgusted with the practices current there. He was terrified to see Buddha in a deeply drunken state, with a filthy smell coming from his mouth, and surrounded by thousands of women. Just at this time there was a voice from heaven, which directed him to follow the customs and practices current in Cīnabhūmi, so that he might obtain final liberation, which was otherwise unattainable. Vaśiṣṭha was mightily pleased to hear the mysterious voice from heaven, and went to the place where Buddha was; and, after being initiated by him, he speedily obtained liberation.[2]

It is needless to point out that the Hindus considered the *Rudrayāmala* and the *Brahmayāmala* as Tantras of the highest authority, and, from their point of view, of highest antiquity. The evidence of these two Tantras and that of the *Tārātantra* clearly shows the Buddhist character of the deity and of the mantra. The Buddhists, on the other hand, attribute their origin to the country of Bhoṭa. But everywhere the mantra is common: Oṁ Hrīṁ Strīṁ Hūṁ Phaṭ. The mantra consists of four syllables, and, as their order is changed, it gives rise to seven more deities named already; and, consequently, if Tārā cannot be regarded as Hindu, all these seven deities, Ugrā, Mahogrā, Vajrā, Kālī,

[1] ibid., app., p. 26. [2] ibid., pp. 29–30 (app.).

Sarasvatī, Kāmeśvarī and Bhadrakālī, forfeit their claim to be called Hindu. It is, therefore, easy to imagine that Kālī, Tāntric Sarasvatī and Bhadrakālī, the three chief forms of Tārā, are all Buddhist in origin, though widely worshipped by the Hindus.

There are fifty-two places considered especially sacred to Kālī, and pilgrimages are oftentimes made by Hindus to these sacred places, and many hundreds and thousands of animals are sacrificed before the goddess even at the present time. It is said that Kālī can only be propitiated by offerings of animals, and, therefore, the temples in certain seasons present the appearance of a common slaughter-house. It is believed that Kālī can grant all desires, provided animals are sacrificed for her propitiation. Thus she is worshipped and offered animals for success in examinations, in obtaining a child, in relieving women from the pains of labour, for obtaining wealth, prosperity, happiness, for bewitching, for separating two friends, and even for killing enemies. The goddess Kālī, who occupies the sanctum in the temple at Kālīghat, in Calcutta, is regarded as a most powerful deity, and people from all parts of India flock together to pay her their homage and offer animal sacrifices. So this one temple of Kālī has been enough to make the whole Hindu population of India thoroughly superstitious; and, what a strange irony of fate that none of the Hindus who worship the goddess know her to be Buddhist in origin, or realize that the practices connected with her worship are Buddhist Tāntrism in essence.

Sarasvatī is the name of a river, and, because many Vedic mantras were composed and numerous sacrifices were performed on both sides of this river, in very ancient times, the name of Sarasvatī was associated with learning and sacredness. Later on, in the Purāṇas we find Sarasvatī as a regular goddess, with various symbols connected with learning and culture, such as the book, the Vīṇā, and similar things. Sarasvatī as a goddess of learning was very attractive to the Buddhist Tāntrics, who incorporated her into their pantheon, and thus we meet with numerous Sādhanas devoted to her worship. The worship of Sarasvatī that is current in Bengal cannot be said to be in any way Hindu, because, while making obeisance to her, she is associated with Bhadrakālī,[1] which is another form of Tārā, as shown above. There is, however, no reason why Sarasvatī and Bhadrakālī should be connected in this manner, unless they are both regarded as different forms of the Buddhist goddess Tārā. Thus it is clear that Sarasvatī, whom Bengal worships today, is not the Paurāṇic Sarasvatī, but the Sarasvatī of the Buddhist Tāntrics.

It is also well known that those who practise the Tantras look upon the mantras with superstitious awe, and they believe that if the mantra is changed or distorted at the time of muttering, either there will be no result or it will produce great harm. The accuracy of the mantra, therefore, was jealously guarded, and the mantras were handed down from preceptor to disciple, so long as the Tantras were a living religion. The mantra which is not given by a guru, therefore, should never be muttered; because a great sin is committed thereby, so they say. If, on the other hand, the mantra is distorted or changed in any unauthorized manner and muttered, great harm is likely to befall the unfortunate worshipper. When, therefore, deities are borrowed by one religion from another, its followers are chiefly concerned with the purity of the mantra, which they cannot change, and it is precisely for this reason that, though the Buddhist Mahācīnatāra was borrowed by the Hindus with a different name, the mantra remained the same. It would really be a very interesting study, if one could collect mantras from the Tantras of different religions, and discover how many of them are common and what their origins are.

[1] At the time of offering Añjali the following mantra is uttered: ॐ सरस्वत्यै नमो नित्यं भद्रकाल्यै नमो नमः ।

Taking the similarity of mantras as the basis of comparison, let us investigate the origin of another deity, who is claimed equally by the Hindus and the Buddhists. This is the Hindu Chinnamastā, who is known in Buddhism as Vajrayoginī. In the *Tantrasāra* and the *Chinnamastākalpa* of the Hindus she is described as of a very awe-inspiring appearance. She holds her head, which has been severed by herself, in her left hand, and carries the knife in the right, and stands in the Pratyālīḍha attitude. She is accompanied by Ḍākinī and Varṇanī, both carrying the Kartri and the Kapāla. From the neck, from which the head has been severed, of the principal deity issue forth streams of blood, one falling into the mouth of the severed head and the two others into the mouths of the two attendants.[1]

When we compare the description of the Hindu deity Chinnamastā with the description of the Buddhist deity Vajrayoginī, we find the two descriptions identical in all details. It is thus apparent that though the two deities belong to different religions and are designated by two different names, they nevertheless represent one and the same goddess. It is, therefore, necessary to explain the origin of the deity; and in this particular case this can only be done by a comparison of the different mantras of the same deity. As regards the question as to when the deity entered into one of the two pantheons it cannot be easily ascertained. *Tantrasāra*, which belonged to the seventeenth century, is very late; and the *Chinnamastākalpa* is of uncertain date. But the *Sādhanamālā*, in which the description of the Buddhist Vajrayoginī appears, gives valuable data in ascertaining the antiquity of this deity. The Sādhana, in the first instance, appears in a MS. which bears a date corresponding to A.D. 1165. Secondly, Siddha Śabarapā is

[1] *Tantrasāra:* Oriental Institute MS., No. 4995, fol. 309 f., where the Dhyāna is quoted from an earlier work, namely the *Bhairavatantra.* Also *Chinnamastākalpa*, Oriental Institute MS., No. 1692, fol. 36 f. For the Buddhist Dhyāna see *Sādhanamālā*, p. 452.

credited there with the introduction of a new cult of Vajrayoginī.[1] As regards the time of Śabarapā, it needs only to be mentioned that he was the disciple of Siddha Nāgārjuna, who flourished in the middle of the seventh century; and, therefore, must have been a generation later than the latter. If Śabarapā is credited with the introduction of a new cult of Vajrayoginī, it stands to reason that the original cult must have been existing at a much earlier date.

According to the canons of the Vajrayāna, the mantra of Vajrayoginī quite naturally runs as:

ॐ ॐ ॐ सर्वबुध्दडाकिनीये बज्रवर्णनीये
वज्रवैरोचनीये हूँ हूँ हूँ फट् फट् फट् स्वाहा ।[2]

The three Oṁ letters are given to each of these three deities—Vajrayoginī (named in the mantra as Sarvabuddhaḍākinī), Vajravarṇanī and Vajravairocanī; and so also the three Hūṁ letters and the three Phaṭ-kāras. The prefix Vajra in the name of the two deities shows that they belong to Vajrayāna. The epithet, Sarvabuddhaḍākinī, applied to the principal deity, Vajrayoginī, clearly indicates the Buddhist character of the mantra.

In the Hindu literature, however, the principal deity is designated as Chinnamastā, because of her severed head, while her companions are named as Ḍākinī and Varṇanī, with the prefix Vajra dropped in the case of Varṇanī. According to *Tantrasāra*, her mantra is:

सर्वसिध्दिवर्णनीये सर्वसिध्दिडाकिनीये वज्रवैरोचनीये इहावह इहावह, etc.[3]

In this also the three names, Ḍākinī, Varṇanī and Vairocanī, all appear; but why the prefixes are changed into 'Sarvasiddhi' in the first two cases we fail to understand. The change appears

[1] *Sādhanamālā*, p. 456. एवं नन्द्यावर्तेन सिध्दशबरपादीयमतवज्रयोगिन्याराधनविधिः ।
[2] ibid., p. 453.
[3] op. cit., Oriental Institute MS., No. 4995, fol. 312 a.

due to the distortion of the mantra, from copy to copy, made in later times by ignorant copyists, or because at the time of the author the tradition was entirely lost, seeing that Buddhism was almost driven out of India in the beginning of the thirteenth century; or because the Hindu Tāntric attributed far less importance to the mantras recorded in the books than those handed down from gurus to disciples. In the *Chinnamastākalpa* again we find a different mantra:

ॐ वज्रवैरोचनीये सर्वबुध्दिडाकिनीये
वज्रवैरोचनीये हूँ हूँ फट् स्वाहा ।[1]

From this it can be definitely said that the original of 'Sarvasiddhi' in the *Tantrasāra* represents 'Sarvabuddha', as is evident from the 'Sarvabuddhi' of the *Chinnamastākalpa*, and if that position is accepted but little is required to show that the origin of the deity is decidedly Buddhist. The prefix Vajra in a Hindu mantra lends an additional support to this conclusion. Vajrayoginī is called Sarvabuddhaḍākinī in Buddhist Tantras, because she is the consort of Heruka, who is looked upon as the embodiment of the five Dhyāni Buddhas, the group being technically known as Sarvabuddha.

There is a third deity, who is equally claimed by the Hindus as well as the Buddhists. This is Mañjughoṣa. The Buddhists recognize him as a form of Mañjuśrī, the god of learning. Mañjuśrī is mentioned in the smaller recension of the *Sukhāvatīvyūha*, which was translated into Chinese between A.D. 384 and 417.[2] We also find mention of Mañjuśrī in such Sanskrit works as the *Mañjuśrīmūlakalpa*, the *Guhyasamāja*, the *Gaṇḍavyūha*, the *Svayambhūpurāṇa*, and in the accounts of the Chinese travellers, Fa-hien, Hiuen-thsang and I-Tsing, and his images in the different Buddhist schools of art, such as Magadha, Bengal, Java and Nepal.

[1] op. cit., Oriental Institute MS., No. 1692, fol. 2 b.

[2] op. cit., ed. Max Müller, intro., p. iii, note 4.

Amongst the Hindus his worship is still current in some parts of the Rāḍha country in Bengal, and his ritual is found in several Tantras, such as the *Āgamottara* and the *Kukkuṭeśvara-tantra*, as we learn from the *Tantrasāra* of Kṛṣṇānanda. Not only is the deity claimed by the Hindus as well as the Buddhists, but also his Dhyāna in the same wording is claimed by both. Curiously enough, the same Dhyāna can be found in the *Sādhanamālā*; and, what appears to be extremely strange, is that, while the verse is attributed to one Ajitamitra in the *Sādhanamālā*, it is attributed to the highest god, Mahādeva, in the *Kukkuṭeśvaratantra* of the Hindus.[1]

In the Hindu Tantra the mantra of Mañjughoṣa is stated as: A RA VA CA LA DHĪṀ: which is a corruption of the original Buddhist mantra: A RA PA CA NA DHĪḤ; by which Mañjuśrī gets one of his numerous names as Arapacana. This form is called Arapacana, because Mañjuśrī and his four companions, Sūryaprabha, Candraprabha, Keśinī and Upakeśinī, originate from each of the five letters A RA PA CA and NA. The correct mantra, therefore, seems to have been preserved in Buddhist manuscripts, which are decidedly earlier; while in the Hindu Tantras the correctness has vanished owing to the ignorance of the gurus, as well as that of the copyists, who engaged themselves in preparing copies of Tantra manuscripts.

The facts mentioned above lead one to suppose that in all these three cases the deities and the mantras originally belonged to Buddhism, and that the Hindus were indebted to the Buddhists for their incorporation into their religion. It is also certain that,

[1] शशधरमिव शुभ्रं खड्गपुस्ताङ्कपाणिं
सुरुचिरमतिशान्तं पञ्चचूडं कुमारम् ।
पृथुतरवरमुख्यं पद्मपत्रायताक्षं ।
कुमतिदहनदक्षं मञ्जुघोषं नमामि ॥

Tantrasāra, op. cit., p. 368, and *Sādhanamālā*, p. 112.

after the borrowing, they were unable to keep up the purity and the accuracy of the mantras, though they had been partially successful in preserving the correctness of the form of the deities. There is hardly a Tantra in Hindu literature which is not tinged with Buddhistic ideas of Vajrayāna and its leading tenets, including the Mahāsukhavāda, and it is no exaggeration to say that some of the Tantras of the Hindus, such as the *Mahācīnakramatantra*, are entirely Buddhist in origin. It has already been pointed out how the *Rudrayāmala* and *Brahmayāmala*, works of the highest authority and antiquity for the Hindus, are profoundly influenced by Buddhist ideas, and how words of ordinary mortals, such as Ajitamitra, etc., have been put into the mouth of the highest god Mahādeva in the Hindu Tantras. It is thus amply proved that the Buddhist Tantras greatly influenced the Hindu Tāntric literature, and it is, therefore, not correct to say that Buddhism was an outcome of Śaivaism. It is to be contended, on the other hand, that the Hindu Tantras were an outcome of Vajrayāna, and that they represent baser imitations of Buddhist Tantras. One more instance is furnished by the *Bhūtaḍāmaratantra* and the deity Bhūtaḍāmara. The deity and the Tantra are claimed by the Hindus, though their origin is thoroughly Buddhist.[1]

Having established the priority of the Buddhist Tantras over the Tantras of the Hindu literature, it is necessary to indicate certain general principles by which Buddhist gods can be detected and separated from among those already included in the Hindu pantheon. It has already been shown that the Vajrayānists described Mahāsukha as a state when Bodhicitta merges in Śūnya, even as salt melts in water, on the attainment of Nirvāṇa; and to symbolize this they conceived the idea of Yuganaddha deities, or deities in yab-yum, where the male and

[1] See *The Cult of Bhūtaḍāmara*, a paper read before the Patna Oriental Conference, 1930, and published in *Man in India*, 1931, Vol. XI, pp. 83 ff.

the female divinities are represented as embracing each other. So these yab-yum deities are an outcome of the purely Vajrayānic concept, which was absolutely unknown in Hinduism before the Tāntric age, and even now does not fit in well with the Hindu ideas and traditions.[1] If there be any deity of a yab-yum nature in Hinduism, there is a strong suspicion that the deity is of Buddhist origin. When Kālī, for instance, is described as locked in an embrace with the god Śiva, we have at once to regard the deity as of a definitely Buddhist origin. Kālī, according to Buddhist tradition, is Kādi or Kakārādi, or, in other words, all consonants of the alphabet, as the vowels are designated as Ādi or Akārādi; and it is not to be wondered at if a deity is conceived by them as Kālī, belonging to the Yogatantra class, and in whom all the consonants of the alphabet are deified. In the Yogatantra and Anuttarayogatantra, it may be remarked, all deities are represented as embracing their Śaktis and experiencing the bliss of Nirvāṇa.

Another important fact to be noticed, in fixing the origin of deities, is their descriptions. If the names of the deities begin with or end in the word 'Vajra', the presumption is that the origin of such deities is Buddhist. Where gods and goddesses are described as lustful and of a very violent appearance, but internally compassionate, their origin may also be regarded for certain as Buddhistic. When deities are regarded as decked in ornaments or Mudrās composed of human bones and representing the Pāramitās, they may also be taken as Buddhist in origin; and, lastly, whenever gods and goddesses are described as bearing a miniature figure of one of the five Dhyāni Buddhas, Amitābha, Akṣobhya, Vairocana, Amoghasiddhi and Ratnasambhava, on their crown, their origin must always be regarded as Buddhistic.

[1] *Indian Buddhist Iconography*, p. 166, where the significance of yab-yum is explained.

CHAPTER XV

CONCLUSION

SEVERAL times it has been pointed out that the Tantras and the Tāntric culture, which at one time regulated the life in ancient India, did not prove very healthy either for the country or for Buddhism. Too much attention to psychic culture, particularly on the part of the general population, was certain to have its repercussions in all departments of life, and history tells us that such repercussions did actually take place. The result was the destruction of Buddhism and the occupation of the country by the Muhammadans, for the first time showing that spiritual force can be conquered by physical force. The advocates of psychic culture were hopelessly out of touch with the realities of life, and practically destroyed themselves and their followers.

Unduly severe criticisms have been levelled against the theory advanced in the foregoing pages, particularly with regard to the unhealthy influence of the Tantras and Tāntric culture on the general public. It has, therefore, become necessary to state clearly the correct estimate of the Tantras and Tāntric culture, especially from an orthodox point of view. No one will be so foolish as to declare that the Tantras contain nothing but preachings of immorality and all kinds of unnamable vices, and in this work, particularly, such views can never find a place. On the contrary, the Tantras should be regarded as the greatest contribution of India to world culture. The Tantras which are intimately connected with the Rājayoga, as advocated in the system of Patañjali and Haṭhayoga, have shown to the world the correct way of developing mental faculties and obtaining great spiritual powers through psychic culture. If by developing the material resources alone great wonders could be achieved, what infinitely greater wonders can be performed by developing the hidden forces of mind? But this is not easy, it requires concentration of mind to a degree almost inconceivable in modern times, in a regularly chalked out procedure. Moreover, complete purification of body, as prescribed in the Haṭhayoga, is also essential for concentrating the mind. Complete control over breath and over wind in the whole physiological system has to be attained before real concentration of mind takes place. The Haṭhayogins ought to be able to stop for days and months the blood circulation, by controlling the wind that gives motion to the blood, and by stopping the action of the heart and of all other organs except the brain. For controlling the mind the Yogins have to pass days and months without food or water, or even air. And however much as it may seem strange today, there were quite a large number of such Yogins in ancient days; and even in modern days, if a search is made, it will not be difficult to find out at least a few. Such wonders as levitation, atomization, etc., are even today possible by having a control of mind. In fact, all that the physical world can perform, by proper psychic culture the same can be achieved in the mental sphere.

The Tantras begin where Rājayoga and Haṭhayoga end, or, in other words, Tāntric culture presupposes Rājayoga and Haṭhayoga. The Rājayoga and Haṭhayoga give control over the mind and body, and Tāntric practices give different magic powers according as different mantras are practised or different deities worshipped.

Philosophers of every age and country have visualized the presence of inexhaustible energy behind the world structure, and this has been named in different schools as God or Spirit, Brahmā or Śūnya. Yoga means commingling. The individual soul is called the Jivātman, while the highest spirit is called the Paramātman. When the commingling of the Jivātman with the Paramātman takes place it is called Yoga. In Buddhism, particularly in the Tantras, the individual soul is called the Bodhicitta and the highest spirit is called the Śūnya, with the three elements, Śūnya, Vijñāna and Mahāsukha.

Śūnya is the highest spirit and an inexhaustible storehouse of energy, setting the whole universe in motion. Therefore, the chief aim of the Bodhicitta is to commingle with this Śūnya and be a part and parcel of the great energy, eternal knowledge and eternal happiness. This is Yoga.

Every day in our life we are having communion with the Paramātman, and whenever the individual Jivātman is depleted it draws energy from that inexhaustible store of energy. And thus life on this earth is maintained. Sleep is required for every individual; but why should sleep be necessary unless it is for having communion with Paramātman, to draw energy from it and be fit for the next day's work? When a patient is passing through a crisis, either in pneumonia or typhoid, doctors are heard to say that perfect and undisturbed sleep even for a short time will save the patient. And, times without number, it has been seen that patients do revive from a dangerous condition after sleep. The reason is not far to seek. The Jivātman in this case, in his deep sleep condition, draws energy from the highest spirit which pervades everything, and becomes revived. Such comminglings are of everyday occurrence. But this is not called Yoga technically.

Every individual passes through three states—the awakened state, the state of dreaming, and the state of deep sleep. In conscious and sub-conscious conditions the Jivātman does not get an opportunity to have communion with the highest spirit. Such communion takes place only in the state which is called Suṣupti, or deep sleep. The difference between Yoga and Suṣupti is really very little, though to remove the difference great efforts are necessary. In Suṣupti the individual or Jivātman loses all consciousness, and cannot realize or feel that it is having communion with the highest spirit, or that it is drawing energy to recuperate itself. In Yoga the condition is different. Concentration in Yoga produces a condition similar to Suṣupti, or deep sleep condition, oblivious to all surroundings, even the physical body and mind, but the Yogin does not lose his consciousness, but remains conscious throughout the process of the communion of the Jivātman with the Paramātman, and feels a kind of divine joy which words are scarcely able to describe.

The object of Yoga is to obtain emancipation, and if that is not to be attained Yoga certainly purifies the mind and the individual, and harmony is produced in life, and therefore spiritualism is sometimes regarded as an antidote to war.

The above will clearly demonstrate that the highest degree of intellectual power is necessary to follow the path of Yoga and Tantra, and that it cannot be, and, in fact, never was, meant for all. Yoga and Tantra were meant only for a few fortunate persons who were blessed with a high degree of intellectual refinement and power. If Yoga and Tantra are made the common property of all, as it was made by the Buddhists of old, the whole routine of life is upset, and abuses of all tenets follow as a matter of course. It is not necessary to state that this psychic culture appealed to men with striking force, particularly when the masters of Tantra could perform prodigious feats and miracles, and, as such, in the time of the Siddhācāryas the Tantras attracted almost every man without exception, and most of them must of necessity have had to be content with the shadow rather than the substance of Tantra. And, as a matter of fact, owing to the great influence of Tantras in earlier days, even at the present time there are very few Hindus in India who are not following the Tāntric practices in some form or other.

The chief complaints against the Tantra is that it permitted women to enter into its fold for the purpose of Tāntric practices, and therefore encouraged corruption and immorality. Such absurd opinions are held by none except the most ignorant of men. It has already been pointed out that the Tantra was divided into various sections, both in Hinduism as well as in Buddhism. With the Hindus Dakṣiṇācāra, or the right-hand path, is to be followed first, after which Vāmācāra, or the left-hand path, is permitted. In Dakṣiṇācāra strict celibacy, restriction of food, drink, etc., are of primary importance, and when the neophyte is sufficiently advanced he is initiated into the mysteries of Vāmācāra, when women are permitted for the purpose of practising the Yoga together. Similarly, in Buddhism, Tantra is divided into four sections. In the two earlier sections, namely the Kriyātantra and the Caryātantra, strict celibacy and restrictions of food, drink, etc., are enjoined. When this course is complete, the neophyte then can be initiated into the mysteries of Yogatantra, in which women become necessary for the purpose of practising Yoga. It has been frequently seen that there is a class of neophytes whose Kuṇḍalinī is not roused without association with women, and for such disciples the great preceptors prescribed association with women. But it must be remembered that both in Vāmācāra and Yogatantra complete control over the air that is contained within the body is essential, and this is obtained after a long-continued practice of Haṭhayoga, Prāṇāyāma, and so forth, so that the association with women produce nothing but help the initiated in rousing the Kuṇḍalinī power which is contained within the body. It is for this reason that the Tantras are to be taken recourse to when perfection is reached in practising Haṭhayoga, or, in other words, Tantras begin where Haṭhayoga ends.

The power to control wind, which gives motion to every little cell in the body and is responsible for the excretory secretions of the body, is not easily obtained. It requires years of patient and systematic practice according to a highly-complicated and dangerous routine. The practices must be conducted on right lines, under the guidance and control of an expert, because mistakes in the process bring on incalculable harm to the practiser. The Tāntrics say that the practice of Yoga is just like playing with high voltage electricity, and a little carelessness may either bring on death or untold sufferings. It is for this reason that we find in the Tantra a great reverence for the guru, who is compared to the highest Śūnya because without an expert the Yoga path is impossible to follow.

Another great complaint against the Tāntric system is that it advocated idolatry, and therefore it made its followers degenerate into mere idol worshippers. Everyone knows that mere worshipping of the idol produces no benefit, and, even though it may have some influence in elevating the society, it can have no scientific value. It has already been pointed out that this charge against Buddhism has no foundation, and those who talk of idolatry with reference to Buddhism have no real knowledge of its philosophical tenets and doctrines.

To seek an explanation why so many diverse types of gods and goddesses were created and worshipped, or to find out the true foundation of the extensive pantheon, mere literature or reading affords little guidance. Though there is no doubt that certain abstract ideas have been represented by means of symbols or gods or goddesses, the great bulk of deities have originated through quite a different channel. By what method such deities have come into existence can only be explained by Yogins, who have visualized them in the past and even today visualize them while in intense meditation. A Yogin in Nepal explained that when the Bodhicitta, by intense meditation and concentration, produces a condition similar to Suṣupti, or deep sleep condition, in his mind-sky (cittākāśa) appears the form of a letter (germ syllable), which gradually transforms itself into indistinct human form. And after some time this form changes in the form of a full-fledged deity, whose appearance, limbs, weapons, etc., appear to be perfect in all respects. These deities are the different forms of Śūnya, or the highest Spirit—the embodiment of Energy or Śakti, and appear before the Yogin in flashes only when he reaches a certain degree of spiritual perfection. This form of the deity, and the process by which the Yogin visualizes the deity, are then communicated to the pupils, so that they may easily and quickly visualize the deity in question, and attain all the supernatural powers connected with his worship. Thousands of Yogins have thus visualized innumerable deities, who may be compared to the sparks coming out of the divine spirit, or the universal energy, and thus the pantheon of the Buddhists swelled.

The above is what the orthodox Tāntrics think of their deities, and it states the principle underlying the conception of gods and goddesses. Indeed, there are thousands of images of gods and goddesses of the Buddhist pantheon, but no one should think that these images were ever worshipped. These images were designed to supply the aid in order that the neophyte might concentrate on the form of the deity. It is to help concentration, and make the process of visualization of the deity more easy of accomplishment, that the images were made. But today what do we find? Images of gods and goddesses installed in every house, sometimes permanently, sometimes temporarily; they are instilled with life with some mantras or charms which have lost their real significance in course of time Flowers, incense, garments, unguents are offered to these images with great *éclat* amidst deafening sounds of drums and other instruments, and the householder obtains supreme satisfaction, thinking that he has done everything that ought to have been done. In this kind of worship there is no Yoga, no purity of mind or body, and no visualization, and hence it is productive of no value, because it cannot give the worshipper any Siddhi, any bliss, contentment or the visualization of the deity. But this kind of worship is widespread now, and certainly it has its value in its own sphere, but, though Tāntric in origin, it has no connexion with the Tantra. It is virtually the metamorphosis of Tantra, on which has been put a commercial value.

The above further shows that Yoga, or even Haṭhayoga, is not meant for all, as it is expected that only a few can fulfil the condition required in a student of Yoga. When this permeates into the masses, the Vāmācāra is reduced to vulgarity and prostitution, which, instead of rousing the sacred Kuṇḍalinī produces illegitimate children, who form a caste by themselves. This was inevitable, and this is what actually happened in the olden days in ancient India, and this is what is even today happening in Nepal, as also in Tibet. Similarly, when god conception becomes the common property of all, it changes into idolatry and superstition. The Tantra, rightly applied, elevates the Jivātman, but, wrongly applied, it takes vengeance and destroys the Jivātman. It caused the destruction of Buddhism as the greatest spiritual and moral force in India.

It is, however, not the object to emphasize here that Buddhism was destroyed simply because its followers were improperly applying the Tantras, but it cannot be gainsaid that the moral force of Buddhism was entirely spent before the Muhammadan conquest of Eastern India, only to be given the last push by the Muhammadans. The other reason why the Muhammadans specially took upon themselves the unwanted duty of destroying Buddhism may be looked for in another quarter.

With the Buddhists monasteries were a necessity from very early times, owing to the peculiar nature of the restrictions and disciplines enjoined by Buddha on his followers. Buddhism, moreover, had no respect for birth or for the orthodox society, and it was mostly concerned with outcastes or low castes, consisting of original inhabitants of the country not affiliated to the orthodox social hierarchy, and for that reason also separate organizations like the monasteries were a necessity in Buddhism, since its inception. Since the time of Buddha, his followers pinned their faith in monasteries, built new ones, equipped them with buildings, paintings, images, stone carvings, and enriched them to a great extent with the accumulated wealth of ages. Some of the monasteries, with their massive stone enclosures and fortifications, presented the appearance of forts, and, as the monks were all dressed in one particular fashion, they resembled an army of soldiers. So long as the Hindus remained at the helm of political power in India these monasteries, monks, and even the lay Buddhists, were not harmed except on rare occasions, because the Hindu rulers always practised toleration in religious matters, and sometimes even embraced religions other than their own. And hence the Buddhists were safe in the hands of the Hindu rulers, but when the Muhammadans came their chief objective was to loot and conquer. They took the monasteries to be forts, the monks to be uniformed soldiers, and forthwith annihilated them, and Buddhism along with them, and thus indirectly saved Hinduism from further disruption, and helped its followers in consolidating their position.

To Hinduism they could do very little direct harm, as religion with the Hindus was a cottage industry, and to destroy Hinduism it becomes necessary to destroy all villages and cottages and the literature scattered over the whole country. Though conversion by sword was in their militant programme, the Muhammadans did not come with the avowed object of destroying any particular religion as such, and they were satisfied when they could get enough wealth and enough territory by subjugating the different rulers all over India. So the destruction of Buddhism at the hands of the Muhammadans was a mere accident, and a great landmark in the history of the development of the different religious systems.

It now remains to be said that the Tāntric culture is the

greatest of all cultures, because it aims at the spiritual perfection and psychic development of man, and as such no one can deny that the Tāntric culture is the greatest contribution made by India towards the world's civilization. Whenever in future man awakens to the necessity of psychic development or spiritual advancement, or of stimulating his latent magical faculties, all eyes must turn towards this branch of Sanskrit literature, and to those few Yogins India still possesses, for the most minute, thorough, accurate, easy and practical system of psychic exercises ever conceived by man in any country or in any time in history.

INDEX